UNDER THE EYES OF THE GALTEES

The Story of an Irish Childhood

KATHLEEN O'SULLIVAN

JANUS PUBLISHING COMPANY
London, England

First published in Great Britain 1999
by Janus Publishing Company Limited,
76 Great Titchfield Street,
London W1P 7AF

www.januspublishing.co.uk

**A CIP catalogue record for this book
is available from the British Library.**

ISBN 1 85756 426 X

Phototypeset in 12 on 15 Bembo
by Keyboard Services, Luton, Beds

Cover design Creative Line

Printed and bound in Great Britain

UNDER THE EYES OF THE GALTEES

The Story of an Irish Childhood

Contents

1

The Hill of Kilmallock

My first memories of growing up in County Limerick go back to the early 1930s. I was born in 1929, the year of the Great Wall Street Crash in the United States, but my lovely carefree childhood in the heart of the Golden Vale was very far removed from the world of stocks and shares. I just about remember our first home, a little thatched house at the hill of Kilmallock, not far from the racecourse and just a short distance from the town.

In those days quite a few of these houses were dotted around the hill and, for a small family, they were very cosy. I remember the inside walls were kept whitewashed, and, with Hannans, the family that owned the lime kiln, only a mile or so over the back road from the town, we were never short of lime. A bucket of water and lime, covered, always stood at the back of the house, ready to give the kitchen a quick going over. Dark green shutters opened back on the window, with pretty lace curtains nestling in between. On the stone floor stood súgán chairs, often with brightly coloured homemade cushions, and a glowing fire in the grate. A few clucking hens out at the back of the house would be getting louder and louder, announcing that they had just laid their eggs, and a glance up at the ceiling was always reassuring, for there would be a flitch or two of homecure bacon, my favourite, hanging from the large hooks.

Mother's lovely homemade bread, fresh butter from the Cork and Kerry Creamery – a wonderful start to the day, except for the big bottle of Cod Liver Oil. Mother would be busy getting the cork off; a spoonful of this would be under my nose and many a time I tried to back into a corner from it but I always had to take it. A spoonful of jam got rid of the awful taste, and that was the end of the ordeal for another day.

I remember the pump at the hill of Kilmallock; it stood on its platform of stone as far as I can remember. People came to it with white buckets for spring water. I would go with mom or dad on a fine evening to collect our bucket of water and sometimes I would take my panny with me for a drink straight from the pump. A panny was a little tin mug children had to drink out of and, of course, if they fell they would not get broken. Mother would have little fancy pot mugs for us when visitors came or, of course, when you got old enough to take care of your own mug. Mine always had a pig on it.

It was just mom, dad and I at that time. Sunday mornings we went to mass to the beautiful church of Saints Peter and Paul. The great big gates of the main entrance would be wide open and as we walked through, the great bells would peal out. All the ladies would wear smart coats and hats or costumes, smart shoes, handbags and gloves. All would match. Men in their Sunday best suits, sometimes hats or best caps. Some older men wore black, round pot hats, dark suits and in cold weather black overcoats. Unlike the younger men, who would wear matching shirts and collars, they would wear separate deep, very stiff white collars. Little girls would have their Sunday best coats and matching hats, or blazers, summer dresses, straw hats and brown shoes or sandals. It would be white ankle socks or long brown stockings. Little boys would look scrubbed in their Sunday best suits. Lots of the older ladies wore black shawls – their best ones, usually with silky fringes around the edges. They would wear dark, very high-neck blouses with long sleeves; sometimes they called these sleeves 'leg of mutton' sleeves. A long, black, very full skirt with high laced boots, dainty, black and of soft leather, would finish off this outfit. A little black, usually silk, bag with a running string through the top edge was carried on the lady's arm underneath her shawl. You would see them bring their rosary beads out of the bags, also, pretty handkerchiefs. Grand-mother at the bridge dressed like this, with her long white hair all coiled up at the back. She looked lovely, a real lady. Grandma in Ballingaddy had been in America for the first couple of years of her married life, so she was more up to date in the fashion world. She wore a lovely coat with a very deep fur collar. The coat was a very dark green, the fur collar was dark brown. I remember playing with the great big buttons; two, as far as I recall, kept the coat fastened. It was quite long. She also wore brown silk stockings; she was always taking care of them, and dainty brown shoes with cross straps and buttons. Her hat seemed to come down very close to her head. It was dark green and had a veil that came a little over the front of it. She carried a big handbag. It had two big, silvery fancy clasps that were like magic when she opened it. She often let me open it, especially if some sweets were just about to be found inside.

So grandparents from both sides, aunts, uncles and cousins came to visit and that is all I remember of the hill of Kilmallock.

2

Ballinscaula Bridge

I just cannot remember when we moved house to Ballingaddy but mother and I started to spend a lot of time with her parents, my grandmother and grandfather, who lived in a cottage near Ballinscaula Bridge. Uncle Jim also lived with them, but he was out at work all day.

Grandmother suffered a lot with rheumatoid arthritis and could only get about on two walking sticks. She always thanked God for leaving her wonderful eyesight and the use of her hands. She was always knitting or sewing for someone in the family, usually for the 'smallies', as they called the little toddlers or babies.

Grandmother loved all her grandchildren. I remember once she counted twenty-five and more came in later years. When a lot of my cousins came on a visit there would be a long line of children, big and small, waiting to kiss grandmother and whoever the latest baby was they'd be getting a lovely cuddle in grandmother's lap. I am sure lots of my cousins will remember grandmother's wonderful stories, told especially when little ones were very tired after a long afternoon playing out, and trouble was likely to break out between cousins. Hands and knees would be washed and everyone would sit around grandmother's armchair and would soon be lost in a wonderful story. Then we would all be told next Sunday she would have another story if we were all very good and let mothers and fathers put our coats on ready for going home. There would be hugs and kisses and another wonderful visit would have gone.

As children, we thought grandmother had a cure for all our ills. If one of us had a cough, she would soon get busy making up a special cough bottle. Someone would help her up out of her armchair and with the help of her two walking sticks she would make her way to the kitchen table. A special white jug, a saucepan and other utensils would be all spread out on the table. She would squeeze lemons, add brown sugar to the juice, glycerine and normally something else, which I cannot remember but it always got rid of a cough. In the spring time, if we got any sign of a rash, we were given nettle tea. This was the juice strained after boiling young spring nettles. I often went with mother to grandfather's field that was across the road and the railway on the other side. Mother would have thick gloves ready to put on and would also be armed with a small shiny bucket and a big pair of scissors. She would always make for the railway side of the field, for that was where the best young nettles were and she would snip off lots of these until the bucket was almost full, then in we would go for grandmother to admire them; she usually said how lovely and fresh they looked. They would then be washed in salt water, drained and dropped into a pot of boiling water that would be hanging on the crane over the fire. They had to be boiled quickly, then some were eaten as a vegetable instead of cabbage, which was quite nice and tasted a bit like spinach, but the juice I did not care for very much. I would be given my panny nearly full to drink. I remember once pouring a lot of it into Barney the dog's bowl.

Grandmother saw me and said I was a naughty girl but when she saw Barney lap it up she laughed and said 'perhaps he needed it too!'

Being country children we very often got thorns in fingers or knees or sometimes even little bits of glass. For something like this she would make a paste out of a disinfectant soap, sugar and resin. All these would be mixed and blended with a little boiling water in a special little saucepan over the edge of hot coals; then it would form a cream paste and be allowed to cool and with an old kitchen knife that she would have wrapped in greaseproof paper she would spread a little paste on a piece of white gauze and place it over the sore spot. A bandage well wrapped round it kept it secure for a few days. Then, when the bandage was taken off, the piece of glass or thorn would have been driven out of the cut and would be plain to see on the piece of gauze.

However, I am sure grandmother's joy was her summer house. This nestled between two white lilac trees and a very large drooping willow tree with a pretty flower bed on each side. Mother or Auntie Kit would help her up from her armchair and with her two walking sticks she would take careful steps out of the kitchen door, stopping to look at flowers on the nice round flower beds that stood one at each side of the front door, then through a little opening in the wall at the side of the house that led to the summer house. I always walked by her side holding on to her long black skirt, thinking I was helping. Then, when she was settled in her place, I would be asked to be a good girl and run for her sewing basket or knitting bag. My dolls and Barney would settle down near her. I remember her showing me how to make a dress for one of my dolls. Sometimes I would be asked to run in and tell Auntie Kit or mother to bring her box and kneeling mat. They knew what she wanted to do, so one of them would come and help her

down on her knees and with her box of gardening tools she
would tend to the flowers. She was alway full of praise about the
wonders of the garden. I often heard her say these words:

> The kiss of the sun for pardon,
> The song of the birds for mirth.
> You are nearer God's heart in a garden
> Than anywhere else on earth.

Grandmother was a nanny in her younger days, to the Honourable Mary Crawley in her beautiful house at the foot of the
Ballinvrena mountain. Over the years she told me wonderful
stories of those days and what a lovely little girl Mary was. All
the family seemed very nice people too. Once a year all the
servants were taken in a carriage to the races of Barrinstown.
They were able to dress up and have a wonderful day out.

When Mary Crawley grew up grandmother was asked to stay
on to be her companion, so they were very close friends. In
time a suitor was found for Mary and great wedding arrange-
ments were soon in full swing. A dressmaker and her assistant
moved in, working on the bride's dress, bridesmaids' dresses
and so on. The master of the house had his tailor out from
Limerick City. The great house and its grounds had to look at
their best. Of course, in those days the wedding ceremony
would take place mid morning, with everyone fasting before
Holy Communion. The feast all the guests came back to was
the 'Wedding Breakfast'. Grandmother told me she would
never forget all the fine carriages that brought guests back to the
great house that morning.

Then, after Mary's wedding, grandmother's own future
would have to be thought of, so she came back to her parents'
home, Stookeens, Martinstown, just a few miles down the back

road from Kilfinnane, that lovely little town, only a short distance from the foot of the Ballinvrena Mountain. She said she enjoyed being home, able to go about and visit friends. Hints were then being dropped to her; it was quite expected that it would be best if a good marriage could start falling into place. Then one day her mother's father told her that after second mass at the local church at Martinstown on Sunday, a young man from a good family in Bulgaden would be coming with his father, the parish priest and the local headmaster with a view to making a match between them. She was told that the young man's father was the sergeant at the little garda station in Elton village, a few miles away on the main Cork to Dublin road. He had come from Halifax in Yorkshire, England, when he was a younger man and had married the local district nurse, but that his son was more interested in farming and that his parents would like to see him settled down with a good wife. Grandmother and her parents went to first mass on that Sunday and were then busy back at home getting Sunday dinner ready in the parlour for the expected guests. They arrived in a covered car, horse drawn. Her father went out to meet them and brought them in. She was upstairs having a last peep at herself in the mirror. She told me with a smile, 'I peeped over the banister and it was all taking hats and overcoats off.' Then her father went for her and down she came to meet a young man with black curly hair and blue eyes, who later became our grandfather. She said that he was very nice and well mannered. After dinner they were told to have a short walk up and down the road outside the house while the discussion about their future went on inside. After a while they were called in to be told that she would go with her parents and her parish priest and headmistress to grandfather's home in Bulgaden on the following Sunday. Grandmother's name was Kate and in the following week she got a chance to tell her sisters Margaret and Hannie all about him. Then when the next Sunday came, off she went, as arranged, to Bulgaden and this time she met her future mother-in-law, a jolly little woman who looked much younger than her husband and who had been far away from her own family in Co. Cork.

So they hit it off from the start. All the final talks took place that day and the next time she saw grandfather was when her father walked her down the aisle. Unlike Mary Crawley's, their wedding was on a much smaller scale, but she said it was all very nice. He took her in a covered car to Charleville, for the wedding breakfast, and bought her sweets, then they returned to a cottage, which both parents had arranged for them, at Ballinscaula Bridge and their new neighbours welcomed them. Grandfather carried her over the threshold; they had a party and danced and sang most of the night away.

Sadly, grandfather was only in my life for a short while. I remember it being cold weather and him coming in from the field by the railway where he would have been helping Uncle Jim. Grandmother always had clean, warm socks ready for him. I would be told to stand back from the fire, but I would hold my two hands to get warm and then bend down and rub grandfather's shins well. I am sure it did not make much difference but he would go on praising me, saying to grandmother what would he do without me. Mother would hand him a mug of hot soup, then it was the filling of his pipe. He would have long paper tapers in a little canister near him, then he would reach one to the fire and make a quick dash of it to his pipe. Then it would be, as he would say, 'full steam ahead'. I would have my dolls in their cot, dressing and undressing them. He would try to remember their names. Mother told me in later years that he always bought me a doll every Christmas. I was often told that it was grandfather that introduced me to homecured bacon and he was very proud to see I took so well to it.

I did hear that when he got to near early middle age and felt his family were now grown up, every so often he would go to a cattle fair and, if it had been a good day, he would meet an old friend and go on a binge of whiskey. He was looked on by people as a fun-loving, witty man, but I am sure that grandmother found it not so easy to cope with. It seems he had a few well-off friends and when they had a few drinks they would have their arms around each other telling people that their friendship went back to their schooldays. However, living it up for a few days did not make as much a dent on their income as it did on his. Not that he did so badly. I have heard that before the First World War, a few times a year he would get the equivalent of five pounds in dollars from his sister in America. One Christmas when this money came, he went into Limerick, bought various presents for the family and the 'latest in thing' for himself, a Penny Farthing bicycle. I really would love to have seen him on it!

One fine day, he got himself dressed up, got out his bicycle and headed for Charleville town. I am not quite sure but I bet that would be about six to seven miles, up hill and down hollow. Anyway, it seemed he arrived there very pleased with himself. He went into some public house and had a few whiskeys and then decided to ride his bicycle home. When he got out a bit from Charleville he came flying down a hill and could not turn the corner in time. He went straight bang up to a gate, the Penny Farthing was stuck in the gate and he went flying over it and landed in a field. Someone had to bring him home in a horse and cart with the bicycle tied at the back. He never trusted it after; he always took the donkey and cart when he was going to have an evening with his pals. He said the donkey always brought him home. What I did not realise, as a small little girl having fun with grandfather, was that he was now very ill. He was spending more time in bed, and grand-mother and mother were always doing something for him. I would take my dolls and lay them on the bed near him, but he would have his eyes closed and someone would say we must leave him to have a little rest. Uncle Jim and mother, or Uncle Bill, Auntie Kit, Auntie Mary and Uncle Pad, all took turns taking two very large jugs of hot and cold water, towels and all that sort of thing, into his bedroom. I was never let in then and was told to be a good girl for grandmother. But what I did find sad was when one of them went to the washstand by the back kitchen window and took down his shaving strap and other bits and they disappeared behind the closed door, because grand-father always let me sit on a chair near him when he was shaving. I loved watching him when he had his face covered with white fluffy, soapy stuff. Sometimes he would bend towards me and put a blob on my nose. He would then reach up to the top of the kitchen dresser and down would come a little leather folder, out of which would come the long razor. He would hold this by its handle like a knife and rub the blade up and down the large leather strap that hung down by the side of the window, then he would pull all sorts of faces as he worked it around different angles on his face. Great swellings of water would go over his face, then all the bits and pieces would go away until the next morning. I also remember him going to a box in which all his stiff collars were kept and a little box of studs. I knew I was not to touch any of these; my finger marks on these special collars would never do and should I do away with one of the studs 'grandfather would be sunk' (his words).

All this had stopped now and one day the priest and doctor were in grandfather's room together. All members of the family

12

started to arrive. Everyone got on their knees around his bed. I was near mother; she had her arm around me and told me grandfather was going to God. They were all saying the rosary and I felt very sad, but said my Hail Mary out loud for grandfather.

My only other memories of that time are of the wake. Lots of relations of the family on all sides were coming and going as well as neighbours, and people I did not know. They all took turns to kneel by grandfather's bed and say a prayer for him. People were given lots of nice things to eat and drink. I remember sitting with some of my cousins on a long seat underneath the kitchen window. We kept climbing up to have a look out and to our surprise Uncle Jim's horse and trap drew up at the gate and he had Auntie Peg with him. We ran out and got our usual hugs and kisses from her and told her all about grandfather. She looked sad and told us that was why she had hurried home. I remember the big glass hearse drawn by two black horses and two men all dressed in black, with high black hats, arriving at the little front gate. The men looked so high up in their seats at the front of the hearse. Grandfather was taken to Bulgaden church that evening for mass next morning. A long trail of horses and traps, donkeys and carts, followed him to his last resting place at Athneasy near Elton village, his parents' burial place.

That was what it was like in those days. Children were allowed to be part of all forms of family life, from the new baby and all the care it would need, to the sick, the old and the death of someone in the family or of a neighbour. In later years it was wonderful to be able to know what to do and how to be a help to other people.

While mother was helping grandmother I was having wonderful fun in my own way. I had Mollie and Larry to visit, a brother and a sister who lived near grandmother. I would drag my four dolls over the road to their house. Mother could see me from the summer house and saw what I got up to on the way. Sometimes I would climb over the ditch to Larry if he was in the garden or if Mollie and he were chopping down 'sally rods', which they grew at the far end of their field that ran along by the road. They would gather all these long rods in a great big pile at the back of the house, Larry would cut off all the green heads and they would sit on two seats and with two sharp knives cutting the sally rods smaller and shaping the end of each one. I am not sure, but these would be about two foot long then, when they had a pile of these done, they would tie them in bundles and have them stacked up in a house outside and people would come to buy them for use in thatching houses. They also grew sugar beet. This was hard work and when it was time for it to come out of the ground they both would be busy pulling it up and laying it along in rows to dry. It would then have to be stacked by the ditch along the road, until one day a big lorry would come to take it up to Cork to the sugar beet factory.

Like my mother and all country women, Mollie would have a flock of hens, a goat we often chased for milk and a pig in his well-scrubbed piggery. I remember helping Mollie to look for eggs if we thought a hen was laying out and when she made up the special grain meal in hot water for the 'hounger', the name Mollie called whatever pig they had. I loved stirring this up with a short brush handle she kept for this job. Buttermilk from the creamery was also given to the pigs and small potatoes were boiled and chopped up for them too. This was the reason for the beautiful homecure bacon. I would count how many flitches of bacon Mollie and Larry had and would tell them if grandmother had more or less, or whether at home in Ballingaddy we

14

had more or less, or any of the local people, but, of course, Auntie Kit and Uncle Maurice had the most I had ever seen.

Mollie always let me put on her high heels and try on her hats. She had a large trunk upstairs with lots of things she had not worn for years and it was great fun going through it. Larry was very funny and would say something like, 'I thought your mother said you should not climb the willow tree?' or something that I was told not to do, but did. Mollie would say, 'How did you know about that?' and he would say, a horse or a cow, or a goat that was near at the time and saw all, had told him. All small children would stop and think about this for a while and on my way home I would give a look to see if Uncle Jim's horse or anyone's donkey or goat was about.

Mrs Neville at the other side of grandmother's was very nice, also her husband Mick and their son 'young Mick', as he was called. I would pay them a visit sometimes. Mrs Neville always had a tin of nice biscuits. I would go and look in all the hens' nests and the duck house to see what eggs I could find for her. I would lift up the skirt of my little dress and make a little nest in it and bring her in two or three eggs at a time and again I would go with her to visit her pig. She was so funny, for she would talk to the pig and tell it how big it would be if all that dinner was eaten up. Unlike grandmother, Mrs Neville was well able to get about and when there was a wake somewhere she would get dressed up in her shawl and long black skirt and high-laced boots and would look very elegant. Off she would go in her donkey and cart then, when she came back she always called in to give grandmother all the news of people that were there and who had sent their best wishes and what a decent send-off the poor soul had got. I remember once when she was telling how kind the people were at a wake she said, 'They nearly lit the parlour round us with punch.'

15

I think it was at that wake that she got talking to a visiting Jesuit Father and they got on to the next world. I can see her now saying, 'I had to tell him, look here young man, God would not make a place like hell. He gave us all too good a chance in this world to do our share of good.' On Sunday mornings she would be off to first mass and if she did not think much of the sermon the priest gave she would tell him the first time she would meet him! I don't know what Mr Neville worked at in his younger days, but from what I remember, in his later years his wife was very proud of the fine garden he kept.

Once a week he would get dressed up to go down to Bulgaden for his pension. The post office was a thatched house across from the church. It was run by the Sargant family. When Mick got his pension he would then walk close on another mile over to Higgins's shop and public house. He would have a little list of a few groceries he was asked to get and tobacco for his pipe, but sometimes he would meet an old friend and they would have a pint of porter. This did not please Mrs Neville and she would lean over their little front gate waiting for him to return. Everyone that would pass from that direction she would ask if he was on his way home. I remember sitting on the wall near her once when she was waiting for him and she muttered to herself, 'Oh, he is a man of easy money now, so he is, p—g it up against Higgins' wall.'

One day when mother and I came down from Ballingaddy, grandmother was very upset; Mr Neville had died that morning. I remember about that time grandmother and mother giving me a lovely bunch of roses out of the garden and telling me to take them to Mrs Neville and to give her a big hug. After that we got to be very close friends and she often told me about her little daughter Biddy that died when she was young. She would say, 'She will have her dad now to look after her.' Young Mick and Tom, and other members of her family were very good to look after her.

Then I had Cleary's to visit. Their farm was over the railway bridge and in a lovely avenue of trees and flowers. I had to get up on my toes to reach the big knocker on the big white front door. Mrs Cleary usually opened it and asked me in. Mollie and Eileen were going to Kilmallock convent, but when they were home they would take me back to the lovely parlour and in turn would play the piano. My dolls went everywhere with me and Mollie and Eileen would make doll's dresses for me, then we would go out into the kitchen where Mrs Cleary would have made nice cake and Mr Cleary would sit with us for tea. He always called me 'the threepenny bit' and would say, 'I have one here for her but I don't know where she can put it?' I would always pipe up, 'I have a pocket in my knickers,' then he would hand over the threepenny bit. In my pocket it would go and I would have to walk home very carefully so as not to lose it.

Mollie or Eileen usually walked me home and often we would meet their brothers Paddy, Tom, Gay and Liam. They were all so very nice. They were very big, tall men. Paddy would lift me up to sit on his shoulders so I could see over the high railway bridge. Very often if mother allowed I could go with them and Mrs Cleary to milk the cows. I loved the drive on the milk cart and would sit near to Mrs Cleary on one of the three-legged stools that they all sat on when they were milking the cows. I loved this fun. Most people sang while milking. Mrs Cleary always said that the cows loved singing and it made them give their milk better. Then when all the milk was put in the tankards we would drive up the high road and look down on Mollie and Larry's house and the avenue to the farmyard. Milk

17

would be put in the long trough for the calves and by now mother would come for me. I would beg her to let me have a look at the pigs and very often the mother pig would be in a house on her own with her litter of 'Bonnays'. Another great visit had come to an end.

Halpin's, the next farm to Cleary's, was another nice place to visit, but I would go with someone else there, because I was very much afraid of the two Kerry blue dogs. Miss Mary, Miss Katie and Miss Brigid were very nice but Mr Halpin, their brother, would pull faces. When I got new black wellies he called me Puss in Boots, because I was carrying my book of that name and he took it from me to look at and said, 'There you are, that cat looks just like you.' How I did enjoy it when his sisters told him off. They would say, 'You look nice in your wellies. Look at the big, dirty wellies he has got, and he would bring them into the house only for us to send him out to take them off.'

However, he could be nice too. Sometimes when he had been to a fair and sold cattle he would bring me a bottle of O'Sullivan's lemonade. It was almost red in colour, and one of the Miss Halpins would give me two Kerry Cream biscuits. The cream in between the two biscuits that made the sandwich was a deep pink and I always thought these were wonderful. Halpin's also had a lot of lovely eating apple trees, so very often I would get a nice apple to eat on the way home. They sometimes gave mother a box of apples to take home to Ballingaddy. Out of the eating apples she would make beautiful apple cakes and there was always one for grandmother and Uncle Jim. We were also able to pick blackberries that grew through the hedge along the road. Mother usually made jam out of these, and then there were the crab trees. They seemed to grow wild in some ditches. Out of these she would make crab-apple jelly.

By now sadness had hit the family again: my little twin brothers, who seemed to come into my life so quickly, had died. I remember they were very small and the doctor coming to the house in Ballingaddy. The priest baptised them Patrick and John after their two grandfathers. Grandfather from Ballingaddy came, he was a big, tall man and had on his big, black overcoat that he only wore for mass and special occasions. He took out one of the large white handkerchiefs he always had and was drying his eyes with it and talking about them being little angels. Grandmother and Auntie Kit and Uncle Maurice came. Uncle Jim, dad and mother were with the two little white coffins, then they all went off. I wanted to go with them but was told that grandmother would like me to stay with her. When they had gone, I sat on her lap. I was upset for it was all very strange. She told me they were too weak to live and that God had taken their little souls to rest near grandfather from the bridge. I was very pleased about that.

However, it did not seem long to me before a little baby sister arrived, Mary. I was very excited about her. My dolls got a rest for a while because I loved helping mother look after her. When she slept in the day time I would climb up on the mud guards of her big, high, black pram to have a peep at her. I remember asking mother where she came from so quickly. She said that while I was at grandmother's the nurse from Kilmallock stopped her bicycle at the gate and out of her black bag came Mary. I told Mollie Brazil to ask the nurse for a baby one day when she was passing the bridge. Mollie said she would, but the nurse was always in a hurry.

That nurse (midwife) lived in a cottage near Kilmallock. She had a notice on her gate: 'False alarms must be paid for.' She was a lovely woman and often when children would be coming from school, she would call out to some child: 'I have just taken

19

a baby to your house, so be very good for your mother this evening!' We believed that when she was asleep God brought little babies down to her house, and every day she put a baby in the black bag she had on the carrier of the bicycle and asked different mothers if they wanted a baby.

3

Bulgaden School

Well, by now my cousins Nell and Doris were very much into playing school. I kept hearing all about a teacher, Miss Fitzsimon, at their school at the hill of Knocklong. So, when on a visit to grandmother's, usually Sunday afternoon, Nell would take charge of us. Doris, Thomas (Tom), Maurice (Mossie) and I would be put sitting on the low ditch of the little back field and not allowed to move. Nell would jump over the ditch into Mollie and Larry's sally patch and find herself a nice piece of sally rod, then we would be put through our paces. If we could not answer the questions she asked us it was a very cross voice, 'Hold your hands out,' and we got in turn a tingle of the sally rod. Sometimes we would run away and poor Nell would have lost control of her class, but this did not give me a good image of school.

Mother and grandmother started saying to me one afternoon that I should put my dolls in their cot for a rest, then out of grandmother's special cupboard would come a little blackboard and a piece of white chalk. It would then start. I would have to count Barney's legs, how many eyes each one of us had, how many fingers we had on each hand, how to spell very small words and so on. If I did well grandmother would open her biscuit tin and I always got two biscuits, one plain and one fancy.

At last the big day came for me to start school. It was decided I would go to Bulgaden School as it was a handy distance from grandmother's house. I was scrubbed the night before and my hair was put in those awful rags that were twisted around each section of hair lengths, to make nice ringlets next day. I also remember while I was going through that awful agony, dad gave me a penny and Uncle Jim found another one in his pocket for me. So getting ready for school was not too bad after all and I went to bed turning over in my head what I would buy at Higgins's for my money.

Morning soon came: it was up for breakfast, then dressed up in all new underwear and a nice check dress, green and white, with a white collar, that mother had made. I liked this dress very much and now with those awful rags out of my hair mother had made my ringlets look very nice. She put a green and white check bow on top of my head, new white ankle socks and lovely brown sandals and, last but not least, my first school bag. It was small and light, just enough to take the little greaseproof paper parcel containing my lunch and a bottle of milk, which was one of grandmother's medicine bottles that had been well washed and the label taken off. Grandmother had polished a lovely rosy apple for me; mother put them one by one into the school bag and told me I was not to look at them again until the teacher at school told the children it was lunch time. It was all a bit strange, I had never heard of lunch time before but there were a lot of strange goings on that morning, like not being allowed to go out to ride the pig, or swing off the willow tree, all great fun. Before I knew where I was the pony and trap were ready at the little front gate. Grandmother hugged and kissed me and told me how nice I looked. Mother planted me up on one of the seats of the trap while she sat on the seat opposite and got busy with the reins and soon had the pony, Bossie, flying off the road. This would only last for a while. Mother often told me afterwards, that she thought that he liked to show off to Cleary's pony, Corney. I remember in between 'Go on, go on,' to the pony, mother kept telling me how much I would love school and all the new friends I would have and what a big girl I was now.

However, I was not so sure – I really did not have time to go to school. What about Barney, grandmother's dog? I was not allowed to take him with me and then there was Mrs Neville, Mollie and Larry, the Cleary family, Halpins and all the animals I looked forward to visiting. Mother promised me that I could do all my visits in the evening when I would have changed out of my school clothes, and that I would have lots to tell everyone.

We soon arrived at the school gate and I began to eye up my new friends who were also arriving with their mothers. Some came by horse or pony and trap, others by donkey and cart. We were all taken into school to meet the teacher, Miss Carroll, who was in charge of the junior classroom. Mothers said goodbye and promised to be back for us in the evening. Miss Carroll led us into the hall, where we hung our blazers up, then we were marched through the big girls' classroom into her classroom. We were put sitting two at each desk. The girl I was put sitting with looked at me in a very unfriendly way and soon told me how awful I looked with my red hair and freckles on my face. She had long hair too, but hers was black and she had rosy cheeks. She must have thought herself perfect, for every time she looked at me, she would pull a face as if she was going to be sick. I soon had enough of this, because I was never before told how awful I looked. The tears were about to flow when I spotted an ink well with a sliding lid over it in the centre of the desk, so I grabbed one of her hands and trapped her fingers in the ink well. She would not say she was sorry, but we were both crying. Miss Carroll came on the scene. It was our first telling off and apologies were soon being made all round.

I remember enjoying our break at midday. Our bottles of milk, which had been taken up by Miss Carroll, were given back to us and my lunch parcel contained homemade brown bread and butter and some fruitcake all made by mother. We were taken up to the back of the school to the big yard where we were put sitting on a long, very low wall. We all thought this was great – no plates or the fuss of sitting at the table – this was great fun and we all had a good look at what each other had to eat.

Bulgaden School is now over one hundred years old and still going strong. I don't know if anything has been added to the back, but the front is very much the same. It has one front door in the centre. In our day it had a front door leading to the girls' school and a front door leading into the boys' school; two classrooms for the girls and two for the boys. The little boys came to the girls' school until they were about seven years old and then one of the masters would come from the boys' school and march them out through the big girls' classroom back with him. All the girls would wave them off. When the girls had finished in the second class we then went into Mrs O'Brien's big girls' classroom. There was a long desk with lots of ink wells. Each class sat at one of these desks, so that when you moved up a class you just moved back to the next long desk. There were not many children in the school, like all country places, houses few and far between and, of course, some children left our school while still young to go off to boarding schools. We did not envy them because we were very happy at

Bulgaden School. It was in a lovely setting. A great big field surrounded the old school walls. Mr and Mrs O'Brien, headmaster and headmistress had a large house near the school. Mrs O'Brien sometimes took the cookery class to her big kitchen and some lovely dishes were made there. To the back of that house stood Bulgaden Castle, then in ruins, but the stories of princes and princesses and knights in battle could very easily form a picture in our minds.

Lots of visitors came to our school and most of them had been pupils in the past. Some were matrons from hospitals in England or the United States who told us how badly nurses were needed to look after the sick and dying. We also got priests and nuns, hoping to encourage boys or girls into their orders, very often for the mission fields. They told us about very poor, sick and lonely people in lots of parts of the world. We always loved their stories. They took us out of our little country school in spirit for a while, so on our way home from school of an evening we would have a talk between ourselves about what we would like to do to help those poor people when we would grow up.

When we reached the age of seven years Miss Carroll told us that we had now reached the 'age of reason' and that meant we knew right from wrong. The ten commandments were written on the blackboard. We went through them all and their meaning. Miss Carroll drew a line through the ones that related to older people and that left very little for us. Nevertheless, the oncs left were well gone through and we were told that it was only us ourselves that knew what we would have to tell the priest when we went to make our first confession.

So coming home from school that evening my friend Brigid and I sorted out what I would have to tell Father Wall. Brigid had got her Holy Communion for the first time the year before, so she was an old hand at it. She asked me if I had ever stolen anything. Shock, horror, of course I had never stolen anything! She then said, 'What about upsetting Maggie Buckley, when we teased the puck goat?' Oh, I would have to tell the priest that, although it was great fun. A few of us would stand up on Buckley's ditch, put our hands up a bit above our heads and make funny noises. The big puck goat with two very large horns, would come flying up the field and ram his horns at the ditch or gate, and we would jump off and fly up the road. I am sure he enjoyed it as much as us, for it must have been very boring for him being there in that field all day. I know Mr Buckley was not pleased about it because he came back to school. We were made to stand out in front of the teacher, who told us it was very naughty and made us hold our hands out and each one of us got a smack of the ruler. We were all told to tell Mr Buckley we were sorry and that we would never do it again. The fact was that I had upset the Buckleys, so it was a sin that had to be told in confession.

As well as this there was the talk we had at school about being very modest. Well, I had gone through a stage where I knew I was very good at standing on my head. I remember when Auntie Peg was home on holiday and I asked her to watch me at my new discovery and she had a good laugh and told me I was very clever and had asked me to do it for some friends. Soon after mother told me it was silly for little girls and that only babies at play did that sort of thing. So that was all over and long gone, but I did get worried about showing all the Cleary family the pocket in my knickers. That would have to stop, so on my next visit there, when Mr Cleary got the threepenny bit out of his pocket, I went to where Mrs Cleary was sitting and whispered in her ear that now I was getting ready for my first Holy Communion, I must not talk about knickers any more, never mind showing them to anyone. She had a whisper with Mr Cleary, who told me I was a good girl and gave me the threepenny bit and God rest them both, I got a threepenny bit for a long time after.

Miss Carroll took us back to the church. We all sat in a row outside while she went in the priests' part of the confession box. She told us before she went in that we were not to tell her our sins, just to say the prayers before and after.

At last the real confession day came and it was Father Wall sitting there in the dark waiting to hear our sins. We were on our own now. I remember going in, kneeling down and saying the prayers I was told to say and then out came the lot, teasing Buckleys' puck, standing on my head enjoying seeing my petticoat and skirt fall around my face and showing the pocket in my knickers to the Cleary family. Father Wall gave me his blessing. I said a very good act of contrition and he told me to be a good girl from now on. I came out very pleased and thought I had got off very lightly.

Well, that night the bath pan was in front of the kitchen fire. Mother closed the door, something that was rarely done in daylight. She had the kettles of hot water ready by the fire and soon had the bath half full, between hot and cold. Just the two of us there for the big scrub I had to go through and the awful hairwashing. When she rubbed my hair to get the wet out of it, I felt my head was going to fall off and then the awful ringlets. I felt my hair was like one of Hartigans' horses' tails when they sometimes passed the bridge with their tails plaited and looking as if they were tied up in a knot. My cousin Doris once said that was why one of those horses threw off the man that was on his back. The poor horse had had enough of what they had done to his tail.

Well, next morning soon came. I was so looking forward to

wearing all the new clothes mother and grandmother had been getting ready for me, especially the beautiful white dress mother had made. When she took it off its hanger and opened the buttons down the back for me to step into I held my breath. Mother buttoned up the back and settled the lovely white veil on my head and with my new white ankle socks and I am sure it was black patent shoes. I felt wonderful, but fighting off the hunger was not easy. Grandmother told me I would have a good breakfast when I came home, but that it would be nice if I went out to visit Mrs Neville because she was not feeling very well and would not be going to Mass. So off I went. Mrs Neville loved my white dress. I twirled and turned to show it off at its best. She asked me to say a prayer for Mr Neville and Biddy. Grandmother was dressed up in her best long black skirt and best dark silky high-necked blouse and her high-laced boots and big black shawl. Mary, only very small, had a pretty little pink dress. Uncle Jim's horse and trap were ready. Dad and Uncle Jim helped grandmother up on to a seat. Both of them and mother, Mary and I, all got on. I was perched at the front with my dress spread out all over them. We arrived at Bulgaden Church and all the girls in my class were arriving in beautiful white dresses. When we all got off the trap, mother sorted my dress out and handed me a lovely bunch of white lilies that Mary Herhir's father, who was a wonderful gardener, had given me the night before. Mother said that when I came down to my seat after receiving Holy Communion not to forget to say a prayer for Mr Herhir's intention. Receiving the host for the first time was a big worry, but thank God all went well. I am sure it was the first time that all of us had to do something very important on our own. It was a lovely day, pennies came from lots of people and I was full of ideas of what sweets and chocolates I would buy at Meades shop near the church, but mother only allowed me to spend very little. The rest was given to me over the next few weeks.

From then on we had our monthly confession, always Saturday morning. We were now taking our behaviour very seriously, for as Miss Carroll and mother would say, 'You cannot keep being bold and expect a trip to confession to make it all right.' So one Saturday each month all children over the age of seven would either be taken by a member of the family or, if big enough, go on their own to church.

I remember as we all sat in rows near the confessional box waiting our turn, a lovely old man would sit with us. When it came to his turn in, he would go and say 'Good morning Father' very loud. We all sat to hear, although knowing it was wrong. The chatter among us would stop and dear old Jim would start. 'I cursed and swore all round me. Father.' Then the priest's voice. 'But you are very sorry Jim?' 'Sorry. Blast it, why wouldn't I be sorry?' and so on it would go until Jim had finished. The priest usually then said, 'You know Jim you should come the men's Saturday, it's the children's day today.' 'Ah sure, we are all children at heart, Father, but thank you very much and God bless you.' Out he would come and if one or two children were going his way he would give them a ride in his donkey and cart. We had a mission in the parish at one time and at one sermon the Holy Father gave a shock to us all about the horrors of hell. Someone commented to Jim about it and Jim replied, as he lit his pipe. 'Ah sure, you would think he was there all his life he know so much about it!'

At about this time a lovely Columbian priest came to the parish on a visit. He came into our school some afternoons. We loved his visits because he was always so happy and loved music. He would take a mouth organ from his coat pocket and play some lovely tunes for us, also some well-known songs. Some of us passed the parish priest's big grey stone house on our way home from school so this young priest, Father Towner, would walk the long journey with us. He told us his stories of life in the faraway mission fields and we told him stories of everything that happened around Bulgaden. He asked us if we would deliver copies of the Columbian magazine when the big parcel of them came to our school. We would now be able to take over from bigger girls who were very busy with lots of homework or moving off to other schools. Each one of us girls were given a brown paper bundle of *The Far East*. We had to call into houses on our way home from school one evening about every three months. People were very nice, thanked us for doing such good work and gave us two big old pennies. That was what it cost. Sometimes we had to go far in the fields to a farmhouse but we were often given a piece of lovely fruit cake, apple cake or a drink of milk or lemonade to help us on our journey home.

4

The Races of Kilmallock

County Limerick down through the years has been the home of some very well-known race horses. Within a few miles of Kilmallock town, and only a mile or two from each other, there have always been some famous racing stud farms. On our way home from school we passed Hartigan's stud. We often called in to the big stable yard to see the horses; all the stables went round in a big circle. It was a wonderful sight to see most of the horses with their heads out over the stable half-doors. My friend Brigid's father and two brothers, Tom and Sean, were some of the men that looked after the horses. They would be either brushing them, feeding them, cleaning their stables or riding horses out. A lot of work and care kept these people very busy.

Surrounding the big stable yard there were sheds full of bags of oats and other grain for the young horses, barns full of hay, big tanks of water and the saddle rooms where you always got a strong smell of leather. Of course Hartigan's had a big farm of cows, pigs, calves, lots of turkeys, hens and so on, but it was the horses we loved to visit. Master Pat and Master Vince were lovely gentlemen. When a new baby foal was born, one of them or Brigid's father, would take us to the stable, open the door and let us stand there and have a good look at the mother with her new foal. This was wonderful; the little foal would be standing up with its straggly mane, big eyes and long weak-looking legs. Its mother would be watching every move. This held great interest for us, because as the weeks went by, one evening we would see the foal out walking with its mother, and those weak legs would have got so strong.

The Hartigans had land at the back of grandmother's house and a gate just past Mrs Neville's house led the way into that land. So very often in the fine evenings one of them would bring one of these foals, when they were fully grown, for what they called 'schooling', to one of those big fields. The first time the horse would have winkers on its head and very long reins. It would be put trotting this way and that way, for a while, then one day it would come with a saddle on its back, be put through some more schooling and then one of the men would leap up on to the saddle and take the horse for a gallop. I sometimes opened the gate for them when they first arrived. I would then climb up on to the high ditch and plonk myself down comfortably to have a grandstand view.

Hartigan's had many famous race horses over the years but my favourite was Lady Flight. I saw her the day she was born, so when they brought her for schooling it was very exciting. As soon as I had opened the gate for her and her master, I was quickly up on my spot on the ditch to watch her go through her paces. I was very proud of her; she could twist and turn so gracefully, her long legs looked as if she was dancing and when she was taken for a canter, her lovely flowing mane blew in the breeze – it was a beautiful sight to be able to watch. I was often lifted up to give her a pat when she was on her way back home. I heard that she ran in the Derby some time later.

Once when we were coming from school the great Sir Harry Ragg was walking round the stable yard with Master Vince. A lot of famous horsy people visited Hartigan's. I remember one evening when we called in for our usual visit, all these men in light-coloured suits and big broad-brimmed hats were being shown around the stable. They were very nice and seemed to love horses and to know so much about them. Brigid's father told us they had come all the way from Kentucky in America. I remember he said 'The blue grass country'; he said it was called this because the people there were very rich racing people with wonderful horses, so that was an exciting story to take home that evening.

Riversfield was another racing stud, owned by somebody called Files and then bought by Major and Mrs Watt. They were very nice people and had some great horses. The one I remember seeing was Sheelagh's Cottage. Across from their estate was Lord Greenall's estate and very big stable yard. Later it became Lady Lillingstones' Mount Coote. I just cannot remember any of their race horses' names. Harris of Faryfield also had stables. They once had a great show jumper but again the name has escaped me. There were also Ashill Towers stables. Mr Maloney of the castle had a race horse most times. Maddens of the Glen were horsy people, Gubbins of Kilfrush, Ryans of Skarteens, Marshalls in Drumon, Lynch's of Fanstown and Lynch's just across the road from Hartigan's. All these people had race horses and maybe more if I could just remember. The only local jockeys that I knew by sight were Brian Marshall, the two Maloney brothers, Tim and I cannot remember the other brother, and there was a jockey, somebody Hartey, from Drumon.

A day at the races was always very popular in Ireland so, when we as children were told if we were very good on such a day we would be taken to the races of Kilmallock, the excitement the night before would start to build up. Family and neighbours gave us the odd penny and before going to sleep these pennies would be counted over and over. With no carpets on our bedroom floor in those days, just a homemade rug by the bed, if some of those big pennies fell from me in bed, they would make such a noise downstairs, mother would come running upstairs to find Mary and I scrambling around the floor under the bed. Mother would sometimes have to light a candle to find all our pennies then they would be taken downstairs until next day. We would be told if there was another sound out of us we would not be taken to the races but we would still have a quiet creep round the bed feeling for pennies, because mother was so cross with us she would not have given us a chance to count what money she had found. Somehow or other we would fall asleep and next morning it was best behaviour just in case that awful dread would hit us, mother's outburst: 'No races of Kilmallock for anyone that is giving trouble,' but of course we were always taken.

I remember once, dad, mother, Mary and I heading off to the races. As we were on our way to Kilmallock, it became so exciting, everywhere suddenly getting so busy, great big horse boxes would rush past us. They would have honked their loud horns and our pony and trap would have to keep well in to the side of the road, then the lords and ladies and majors, captains and the honourable so and sos, would give us very sharp and loud honks from their beautiful motor cars as they so snootily drove past.

I think of those days whenever I see those beautiful cars, now called vintage cars, when they are shown on TV or in the newspapers. It was a wonderful mixture of the general public. Lots of people would head for the races on bicycles, some people would walk there, some would even travel in their donkeys and carts and I think most went by the horse or pony and trap. People from a bit further away would come on the trains from Cork or Dublin directions and get off at Kilmallock station, then walk down through the town to the racecourse at the hill of Kilmallock. I remember there were places where we could leave the pony and trap and then we would walk up the hill and on to the racecourse. All the bookies would have set up their stands. They looked very colourful in bright check suits and big hats. They would have all sorts of coloured posters relating to the names of horses and to betting on them and would be shouting and waving their arms all about the place, telling what odds they would pay on such and such a horse. All along one side of the big field would be the big horse boxes with the backs open down to the ground. The race horses would have been walked very carefully down. A group of people would be around each horse: the owner, who was very often the trainer, a couple of grooms and the jockey, and maybe a few other people concerned with the race horse. Everyone of them would be fussing about a lot. One day a lord so and so was getting very excited about his horse and was shouting orders to his group of people. For a second he had lost sight of his principal groom. He shouted, 'Where are you so and so?' The reply came, 'At the back of your n'arse my lord.' 'Oh, jolly good,' was my lord's reply.

Jim Denine's tent was the place we had our eyes on as a place to spend our pennies. Jim had a nice shop in the town where he sold rosary beads, prayer books, pencils and exercise books for school, but most important of all he sold sweets, chocolate and sticky buns of all kinds and, of course, the wonderful O'Sullivan's lemonade. So his tent at the races was the place to feast your eyes while clutching those pennies. I remember once, we met

Uncle Bill and he gave Mary and I a sixpenny piece each. We could not believe our luck. We had a ride on the swinging boats and bought lemonade and chocolate, a halfpenny bar each. A lady and gentleman from Charleville always had a lovely tent where they sold the most beautiful oranges and apples. So on that day we were also able to buy an orange each and one to take home to grandmother. Mother took charge of the chocolate and saved some of it for us the next day. There was also a gipsy caravan, but we were not allowed in there. Then all at once all the people would be rushing up to the hilltop, a sign that a race was about to start. We children would be hurried along. Dads and uncles would lift us up to sit on their shoulders to watch the race. We would watch the jockeys ride their horses to the starting post, then the shout would go up 'They're off.' It was great watching them clearing fences away in the distance. They would take a big turn, almost a circle, before turning to run straight up in the direction of the hill to the winning post. Everyone would be shouting and jumping up and down with excitement particularly if their horse was in the first three. Of course, some people had the winner and others were not so lucky and then the bookies would have their big bag of money ready for paying out. Some people would have quite a few of the lovely big green pound notes to collect. Others a few of the old, almost orange, ten-shilling notes to come.

It was at the races of Kilmallock that I first saw the lovely old five-pound notes, with the black and glint of gold on a white background. They looked like a piece of parchment. I remember one gentleman that we knew well asking us if we were putting our pennies on a horse and he was joking with a very jolly bookmaker called Paddy Stack. He then took his wallet out and said, four fivers on such a horse and when the race was over and the horse had lost I thought he would have been so upset, but not a bit, it was wallet out again for the next race. It was a lot of money in those days but I expect it was not much to him because he went about quite happily for the rest of the day.

Well, the last race was run, and everyone around us was packing up to go home. I always hated this for it meant the races of Kilmallock were over for another long year and that was the only racecourse we were taken to. We would hear people talking about races in other towns such as Bruff, Clonmel, Tipperary, the Limerick Junction, Buttevant, Limerick City, Galway and maybe more down the county. I am sure I heard of the races of Killarney, then there were all the racecourses up near Dublin.

I always took grandmother an orange from Kilmallock races because she said that was one of the first things she'd bought when they had had that wonderful day out there, when she was looking after Mary Crawley.

I do hope that one day before I get too old I may find myself at Kilmallock races again. Please God.

5

Lissacorra

The house we lived in at Ballingaddy was called Lissacorra. Dad was a caretaker for a Mr Rohan that lived out somewhere in the County Cork. It was a very large farmhouse. Most of it was thatched, just one small section slated. There was a very large beautiful parlour and a couple of lovely bedrooms that were out of bounds to us. Mother just kept them clean and dusted and the doors were kept closed all day. Sometimes when Mary and I were playing out and the bottoms of the windows were lifted up we would scramble up to the ledge to have a good look around the parlour. I always had to lift Mary up to get this view. One day she reached in too far and fell in a heap on the beautiful carpet. I had to go and confess to mother what happened, so she had to get a key and unlock the door to get Mary out, who by then was all hot and clammy from crying. I got a couple of smacks across the backs of my legs and we were told that if we ever climbed the windows again she would lock us both in there for good. So of course I promised never to do it again, then we were told to dry our eyes and she took us in to the beautiful parlour and let us have a good look at everything and then the bedrooms. She told us if we were very good she would take us in again; she kept her word, something that dad and her always did. But I think we lost interest in that part of the house.

The rest of the house had plenty of space for us and a lot of land went with the house. Mr Rohan kept lots of dry stock (cattle) on his land. Every so often he would arrive in the yard in his new, big, dark blue saloon motor car. As instructed by mother as soon as Mary and I saw the first sign of his car, we ran behind the half door, that all farm houses had in those days, leading in to the kitchen. We watched all the clever twisting and turning he could do with the car from our safe spot. He was a very nice man, quite big, always in a navy suit and a big hat. When he finally came to a standstill he would open the door and heave himself out. He always came and had a chat with us, especially Mary who was into very funny chatter at that time. Every so often he would bring a drover, a man that drove a large amount of cattle along the road in front of him, to a fair in the town or wherever he was asked to take them. They would block a road for ages. All these cattle would keep passing and you would just hear the drover's voice keeping them on the move. Every cattle dealer had his own brand marked on each beast and a lot of country people would know the owners of each herd. These men always seemed to wear long overcoats or lightweight raincoats and a peaked cap pulled down at one side. They usually kept themselves to themselves and just got on with their job. I remember some big outhouses at Lissacorra – they had big containers for the food for the cattle and each had a big loft full of bags of grain. Dad had to bring these down on his back, I think it was each night, to be got ready for their food next day, especially in the winter time. And then there was all the farm work that had to be done, because dad had his own main job to do, which I will tell you about later.

It must be at about this time that Grandmother Ballingaddy

died. I do not remember much about it because she spent a lot of time with her eldest daughter, Auntie Peg, in Buttevant and I think she must have died there but it was a sad time. Auntie Norah, Auntie Mary Ballingaddy, as we called her, Uncle Jerry and Uncle Mick and poor Grandfather Ballingaddy all came in to us and I remember hearing them talking about when they were all young. Grandfather then lived on his own in a cottage very near the very long boreen that led into Lissacorra. He would tackle up his donkey and cart to come in. He was a fine man and very independent. I am sure all his family worried about him, but seeing we were the nearest, he would come for meals sometimes and liked talking everything over with dad and mother. He often said to mother, 'Hannie, you would make the grass grow if you thought it would help someone.' I remember once, we brought grandmother from the bridge up to Lissacorra. I think it was only the first time she came. She just could not believe any house could be so far in from the road. As we turned in the boreen from the road we had a long drive in the pony and trap until we got to the first big, white gate. I got off and opened it wide and when mother had driven through, I closed it, then it was a long drive to the next big white gate. Off I got again and did the same. Off again to the last big wooden, white and black gate and it was only then the big house came in view.

Grandmother said it was like where the Green Man of Wisdom lived, where sun or moon never shone. Even the travelling people did not come in very often. I know they are called beggars these days. They kept themselves clean and only wanted a place to put their head down at night. A meal or some food always came in handy. When they would be leaving they would bow their heads in prayer for the dead of your family and for good luck to everyone in the house and thank you maybe

41

for a meal or a night's sleep in a barn or outhouse. Mother always had a couple of blankets, a quilt and a pillow standing by ready for them. Dad could be very kind to them too, but always tried to make us think that he was not going to be soft on them: 'Bastards, that some of them should be doing a day's work.' Mother would make the sign of the cross and say, 'God forgive you, sure we don't miss the bit we give them, and some of them are getting old now.' He would go off talking to himself and when we would look later he would have a bed made up for one of them. Mother would give him a kiss on the cheek and say, 'We will all be hoping for a bed in heaven.'

We met one man, Paddy Supples, near grandmother's one day and mother said, 'Paddy, why have you not been in to Lissacorra to see us?' 'Ah, sure missus, how can I get in there with my two bad feet?' Mother said she was so sorry to hear that but that she had some old clothes of grandfather's and dad's and that she had done some shortening in trousers and so on. So she promised to leave them at grandmother's for him. He was delighted and said lots of prayers there in the road for us.

Kate Crow was one of the travelling ladies. She was the only one that came in to Lissacorra. She was like another grandmother to us. She always had a neat shawl, black skirt, and a pretty flowery-patterned blouse. She also wore a big, striped apron. This would be quite colourful, it had two big pockets where she kept all the pennies she had begged on her travels. Once, Mary was near her and started patting those two, big pockets and started to shout, 'Pennies, pennies.' Kate was saying, 'Go away little girl, go away now and play.' Mother had to drag Mary away. These people always had a bag with all their bits and pieces. Mother always let Kate sleep inside the house, she was so very clean and neat. I think she had a little house in some place in Cork and when she found herself with no family she started travelling the roads but went back to her little house in the winter. She would stay and do a fair day's work for people if they were very busy or if someone old was not feeling very well. She was very honest and could be trusted wherever she went. She often said, 'You will never get a smile from the boss behind the clouds if you take what belongs to someone else. Remember that little girl. You don't learn to be honest and truthful at a grand school, you learn that at a good mother's knee.'

Well, our time at Lissacorra was coming to an end and I was glad because we were so cut off from everyone. If it was not for the time spent at grandmother's at the bridge and Bulgaden School, life would have been very dull.

6

Our New House

Our new house was built and ready for us to move in. It was a bright, cheerful bungalow on the Kilmallock to Kilfinnane road, just a short distance from Ballingaddy Church. At first it looked strange perched in the middle of a field, a high ditch with wild bushes along the front. Two little outhouses around the right-hand corner, one a chemical toilet, the other for whatever use we thought best, but I shall never forget when mother and dad took us around the back of the house and pointed out to us the wonderful view. As I looked across the large span of mountains, dad pointed out the Blackrock mountains, the Ballyhoura mountains and on the far left the Ballinvrena mountains.

Over the years they held such a dreamy wonder. Their colours changed with the change of weather. Sometimes on a fine day they gave us a range of rich greens, and on a gloomy day the picture was ranging from light blue, very deep blue, almost navy, mauve and purple. Mary and I and, in later years Peg, loved to sit on the ditch and point out to each other the different houses, big and small, we could see up the winding mountain roads. We would wonder if children lived in those houses and where they went to school and wondered what it must be like living in a house that looked as if it was hanging on a cliff.

Grandmother, mother and Auntie Kit were great storytellers about the people that lived in the mountains. I remember my cousin Hanna May, who was the same age as Mary, loving those stories, for when a story had come to an end, she would say, 'But what happened to them then?' And Auntie Kit would say, 'They are all gone to bed now and we must get the horse and trap and get off home to bed ourselves.' They would all pile on the trap and we would wave them off until another day.

Poor dad's mind was busy planning the layout to change the image of our new house. He had to get rid of the big ditch and all the wild bushes. He got a little help from the men of the family such as Uncle Jim, but every man worked such long hours up to Saturday night in those days, that he had to do a lot of it himself with a little help from other. He laid out nice cement paths from the front door out to the new small gate and piers, and lovely long walls in front of the house. Two large piers and a white gate at the very end on the left hand side for the horse and that sort of thing to go in and he laid out a nice passage to the back of the house. At first we had two green lawns at each side of the path at the front. Wonderful for us to tumble and play.

By now we had a new sister, Margaret. Dad would sit her on his knee and sing 'Peggy O'Neil', so it was not long until she was called Peg and that has stuck to her ever since. Mary looked on her very much as a plaything and could not understand why babies had to sleep so much. I now felt quite grown up and enjoyed helping mother with them both, Mary in particular. I would drag her out to play while Peg had a sleep. Everything had to be planned, there was always plenty of work to be done.

Dad had his garden in full swing. Mother had a flock of hens and chickens, lots of rose trees were planted, the flower beds had started adding colour and the place looked as if we had been there years.

We had nice neighbours. The Hennessy family had come to their new bungalow across the road from us. There were very nice girls in the family, all very pretty. I am sure they had just one brother, Paddy. Mrs Hennessy, like mother, would have a long washing line of little girls' clothes and they only had the old flat irons in those days. They usually had two on the go, one in the big open coal fire getting hot and the other in full swing doing the ironing. We all wore white or cream starched petticoats. The white blouses for school had to have some starch in or they would not look fresh and crisp. White collars to summer dresses would be starched, not to mention all the starched white collars for grandads and coloured collars for the younger men. All the white ankle socks had to be boiled to get shoe or sandal marks out. They would be in a big pot hanging over the fire, with what we called a possing stick, bleached white, ready on hand to give them a good possing around the pot of soapy water. We had no well-known brands of soap powder, it was a pound bar of Sunlight or carbolic soap. Mother would have a special knife to slice off the bar the amount she would need; this would be melted in a little warm water before being added to the pot of water. The same boiling was done to white blouses, or whatever else was white, and was to be brought up to look snow white and they always did, and certainly were 'whiter than white'.

I think the first advert I saw was up on a board near the Picture House, as the cinema was called. It was of a lady fast asleep in bed and another picture of one of the old bath pans full of clothes steeping over night. The words underneath 'Sunlight is at work while you are asleep.' Adverts have gone a long way since then.

7

Dad's Job

Dad was a postman, but not one that came with letters in the morning. His day started at 4.30 a.m. and his job was a contract with the post office, which meant he was responsible to supply a good, strong, well-kept horse to draw the big green post office van. It also meant that all the leather tackling for the horse had to be in tip-top condition. They gave him a uniform and his book of rules and regulations which he always carried out so carefully.

The reason for his day starting so early was that, after he got up and had had a quick breakfast and had tackled up the horse and van, he would sit up on his high seat at the front and drive down to Kilmallock railway station and collect the bags of mail that came off the train from Cork and Dublin later the night before. He would take them to Kilmallock post office where they would be sorted out. A collection of mail would be ready there and added to any that had been sorted from the post he had collected from the station. He would then drive up to the little town of Kilfinnane. We were about two miles from Kilmallock so I am sure his drive from Kilmallock to Kilfinnane would be at least five miles, most of it up very steep hills. He would hand over the post bags, registered letters and valuable post packets and parcels to that post office. He would then collect the post from Kilfinnane post office to take down to Kilmallock railway station for the early Cork and Dublin trains and then continue down to Kilmallock post office with any mail that was for the morning postmen to deliver around the town and out in the countryside. I am not quite sure what time he got back home, sometime mid morning, and with not having the worry of looking after the cattle at Lissacorra any more, he would do a few hours' work around the new house after a short rest and a good meal. In the evening he had to tackle up the horse and van and go through much the same performance on the post as he had done in the morning. So by the time he had finished that round it was late when we heard the clip-clop of the horse and the heavy thud of the van as soon as he turned the bend of the road just past Ballingaddy Church. It was nice on the bright nights to see him coming along, but the dark nights, that can be so dark on the country roads, were a different matter. When we went in turn to the right end of the house we could see very little of the van, horse or him. It was just the clip-clop, the heavy thud and the two lamps that hung at each side of the high front of the van giving a glow that kept moving nearer. They looked strange being so far apart in the dark. It was as if the two lights were dancing down the hill.

Mother always seemed to go out to meet him. Sometimes he may have had shopping from Kilmallock for her that he had picked up earlier. I often think now that when he got himself down from that high van, especially on a cold winter's night, he never greeted us with grumbles, but was always interested in what we had to tell him. First thing was to look after the horse. He would be untackled from the van, brushed and fed and in the winter put into a nice clean stable. On summer nights, he was let out in the field. Of course, the van too had to be kept clean. A large pot of water would have been kept warming by the open fire. He would tip it into a bucket, mother would have old cloths ready for him. Out he would go and, with the light from a lantern, he would wash the fresh mud of the roads off the wheels. The two lamps of the van had often to be made ready for the dark of the next morning. It was only then, when he had a quick wash himself could he call his 'soul his own'.

The supper table would be laid ready. Always mother's home cooking. Dad would have taken his place at the head of the table sitting there in trousers and shirt, collar and tie taken off, just a big pair of braces standing firm over his shoulders. Whoever was the baby or toddler was perched up at the table between mother and himself and he would take great pleasure feeding the little one. Then mother would take whoever it was and dad would look around the table to talk over the day. I always sat at the foot of the table and for a while there was just Mary sitting opposite mother, but later on there were a lot of us around that table. Everyone had their way and everyone was listened to. Mother and himself would discuss money matters, such as, who would need money for school books, jotters, pencils, exercise books. Someone might need shoe repairs, new shoes, money for some particular thing at school. They were both wonderful managers with the little money they had. We never went short of what was necessary for us. Maybe we were lucky to live in the country where people were either self-sufficient or very rich and we knew as children which group we belonged to and we were quite happy with that. Dad always seemed happy with his life. Just the odd outburst now and then about something. He was always very good at letting someone tell their side of a story and so was mother and I am sure that was why they had such a wonderful marriage.

After supper dad would make himself comfortable by the

fireside. Now that I was the big girl of the family I would clear off the table, wash up and put everything away carefully in their places. Mother would be scrubbing the little ones. They would be perched up on súgán chairs in front of the fire in their nightdresses. There would be a little short prayer said that they could follow, then kisses all round, a sprinkling of holy water for the 'poor souls' and off to bed.

I then felt very grown up. Dad, mother and I would be settled on our chairs around the fire. Mother would sometimes read from a good book. This was always nice and we would look forward to following some story. Other times she would have her sewing machine up on the kitchen table, usually finishing off a dress for one of us. Sometimes a light knock would be heard at the door and one of the neighbours would walk in, always a man. He would remove his hat or cap and say 'God bless and save all here.' The reply from the fireplace would be 'Ah, sure God be with you, drag up a chair and sit down.' Then the grown-up chatter about places, work, farms and weather. It would not be long until mother would say, 'It is Betty's bedtime, so with God's help we will get on our knees and say the rosary.' Mother went to the dresser and got out dad's, hers and my rosary beads. Our visitor would very often take his own out of his pocket, but if it was a young man, mother usually found him some beads even if she had to do a running repair in them before handing them over. She knew I always lost count though, letting my mind wander. I would be soon brought back with a nudge and a loud 'Glory be to the Father.' Then we would have to go through all the trimmings after the rosary. Special prayers for the sick people we knew, people that had died lately. Sometimes dad and the visitor would be slumped on their knees over the seats of the chairs and beginning to snore. Mother would wake them up and say,

'What a picture Our Blessed Lord had to look down on tonight!' I would have to go to bed, but I would have seen the kettle singing over the fire and heard the rattle of mugs and tea being made. I did not like missing them, I knew they would be having some sweet cake to eat. In later years I was allowed to join in that special night treat.

Winter nights were cosy around the fire, but summer evenings when it was light until so very late, I am sure made poor dad's waking day even longer, because after supper he would have a short sleep in the chair by the fireplace with his shoulder leaning to the chimney breast. He would wake up and have a last look round the kitchen garden, checking the different vegetables and, if a weed dared to show its ugly head, he would soon be after it. He had high mesh wire around that garden and sometimes hens would find a place to get in through it and do some scratching. This he did not like and as a very small little girl Peg was aware of that, so in the daytime she watched the hens and what they got up to for him. Sometimes when we were in the house we would hear the very excited clucking of hens from the back of the house and looking out the back window a chubby little girl could be seen giving chase to the poor hens. Mother would run out and say, 'Stop it at once Peg, you will chase them so much they will not lay any eggs!'

8

What We Did for Entertainment

I just cannot remember what year it was, but I am pretty sure it was before I started school, that dad took mother and I to Fyons to see the great Clipper. I think we must have gone in the horse and trap to Uncle Bill's in Drumon near Bruff. I think we then went on what they called a charabanc the rest of the way, but there were crowds of people, and the estuary of the river Shannon looked enormous. We did not see the people get in of course, but it rushed very quickly along the water and sent a great spray into the sky. A lot of talk went on all round us, but it was supposed to cost a lot of money to go to America that wonderfully fast way, not like the ships early on that took six weeks. Mrs Neville, that lived near grandmother, was taken to Fyons by her family as a day out. She watched the great Clipper in wonder and when it disappeared up into the sky she said, 'Oh dear, a call will not bring them back now.' So it was only the Irish people who had emigrated to America that had good jobs, well settled, and had plenty of money, that could travel in the Clipper.

We did not travel many miles from home in those days apart from visiting family and friends. Another place I can recall often being taken to was to the Blessed Well of St Malou. It was not very far from Martinstown Church. The legend was that years and years ago the well was in a farmer's land and people believed it was blessed water and had every respect for it and would come to pray there. One day a tinker woman started doing washing of clothes in the well and when the farmer told her that it was a blessed well, she took no notice but carried on. The next morning the well had moved to another part of the field and the old one had dried up. Grandmother had great faith in that blessed well, so Auntie Kit or my mother would take her once every year, usually on a Sunday. It must have been on the feast day of St Malou. Women and men would say lots of rosaries, children a Hail Mary. There was a big bush near the well full of coloured ribbons. Everyone that visited tied a ribbon on the bush. Some ribbons would be faded, others would look new and bright.

The fifteenth of August brings to mind the Pattern of Ballylanders. Although I was never taken there, I well remember people going. Lots of them went on bicycles and that day out seemed to mean a lot to them over the years. We were often brought back sweets and long strings of Black Jack and a cane of sweet called Peggy's Leg.

Some nights our school was used as a library for adults. At one time Larry Brazil was in charge of it. Uncle Jim got great pleasure from Bulgaden library, but the war years spoilt this for country people; the half gallon of paraffin oil having to be used very sparingly. I remember Sunday afternoon was very much the time to get down to a good book for a lot of people.

I well remember another way of socialising for men was collecting in groups at Ballinscaula Bridge, the long lower bridge down from the railway bridge. They would lean over that bridge chatting for a few hours and with the bridge being

up high they had a wonderful view of the Ballinvrena mountains and could see fields of all shapes and sizes rising for a long
way in front of them, from fields full of rows of different crops
to beautiful fields of golden corn. Then, of course, they could
look down on the lower road, but there was not much passing
on the roads in those days, although that lower road was the
main Cork-to-Dublin road. A motor car that passed would be
watched out of sight. Someone riding a horse or a bicycle
would stop and have a chat with them and they seemed very
happy. Although there was the odd public house within a mile
or two it did not seem to draw them. I did hear that on a dark,
winter's Sunday night a couple may go for a pint of porter to
Higgins's in Bulgaden, and a few more may walk the couple of
miles to Elton village that had three public houses, Jones's,
that in later years became The Cosy Kitchen, Crowley's, and
O'Sullivan's, which was also a fine grocer's shop. In these pubs
they could sit around a fine blazing fire.

They were all nice people that owned these places and they
were very homely, no pressure to drink too much because each
landlord did not have to rely on the pub for a living – they
usually had a shop or some other business as well. So the pub
seemed as if it was a service for local or passing people. Paddy
O'Sullivan was very popular with some men from the surrounding
area for a drink on a Sunday night. When they would be leaving
for home at closing time he would walk to the door with them,
wish them good night and always said, 'Straight home now and
keep the middle of the road.' With no cars on the roads in
those days, the middle of the road was the safest place for
them, because if they walked near a ditch they might stumble
and fall on very uneven ground, or may get tangled up with a
couple of goats asleep by the roadside in the dark, and a puck of
one of those hooves was no joke. So that kindly warning was

something to remember on the long dark road on the way home. Mr and Mrs O'Sullivan were two very nice people. I always liked going in their grocer's shop. They brought up a wonderful family. I know they had a lot of sons that went into the priesthood and I remember hearing in later years that those priests had risen to high status in the Church in different parts of the world. I think it was son John Jo that kept the name of O'Sullivan over the door.

I think some few men from the bridge on fine summer evenings would go to Higgins Cross to play Pitch and Toss, but men did not have much spare time in the country in those days. They were up very early in the morning, cows had to be milked, animals had to be fed and there could be a lot of them. Milk had to be taken to the creamery, crops had to be planted and without motor-driven machinery it could be walking behind a horse and plough for hours on end. Hay cutting and saving and driving home to the barn was also hard work and then there was wheat, barley, all harvest crops which entailed a lot of work. The threshing machine was very much a case of all hands on deck when it hired itself to some farmer for the day. It was very nice because all farmers and their sons would just go from farm to farm to help each other on the day of the thresher. Women would also help each other out with the large amount of food that would have to be cooked on that day. There would be sides of beautiful beef, hams, the good old homecure, with beautiful fresh home-grown vegetables. A barrel of porter would have taken up its position in a corner. There was a crate of O'Sullivan's lemonade and a lot of us children on our way from school were invited to have one with cake, biscuits or a piece of apple tart, which was wonderful. What wonderful grown ups we spent our childhood with. They never grumbled at us when they were working so hard, but were so grateful to be able to save their crops in good weather. I remember the Protestant minister in Kilmallock was having a hard time trying to get his hay saved before the weather broke. Our parish priest must have heard about it, so on Sunday morning at first mass, he stood on the altar steps after the sermon and said, 'Canon Taylor has a field of hay down. I know it is Sunday but the good Lord would think it best if you young lads got your coats off and got it finished for him today,' and they did.

Another form of social life for grown ups in the country on winter nights was 'the gamble', more so before the war. As children we would hear people saying there would be a great gamble at so and so's tomorrow night. I remember getting the gist of what they were talking about. It seemed older men sat round a table in someone's parlour playing cards; no money would be played for. It was always for a turkey, a fine fat one, and it was always weeks before Christmas. Then the big kitchen would have been made empty, the only thing left in it would be the big dresser with all its big dishes and fancy pots. Some local person that played a piano, accordion or a violin would play dance music for the young people. They had the kitchen to themselves. Mollie Brazil, who explained it all to me, said it was great fun. The music man would be calling out the dance steps and all the twists and turns of the dance, so when they were all lined up to do the Walls of Limerick, he would say what steps they started with and while playing the tune he would shout, 'Right around the kitchen and mind the dresser!' In later years these are the words a band leader would use in a dance hall putting young dancers through the Walls of Limerick. The people playing the cards and the young couples that came for a dance and a chance to see a young girl or young man that they had their eye on, all paid only about a shilling for the great night out and there would be a good supper. Young people of my age missed out on those years but they must have been great fun and many a romance started in those local kitchens that led to a wedding.

The lords and ladies too were very good to let their staff have a big party once a year. They could invite friends or brothers or sisters. They not only had wonderful eats and drinks but each great house had a beautiful ballroom for dancing and a band would have been booked for the party. The lord and lady would join them sometime during the night. Again, war years did away with that, all but Lady Lillingstone, the new lady in Mount Coote, she kept them up for her staff.

Mothers and grandmothers that were fit and well able to walk would visit each other, have a nice cup of tea, a special cake and a good chat about babies and schoolchildren and exchange knitting ideas, sometimes bringing their knitting with them. When I was a child women seemed to be always knitting men's socks and long black stockings for their daughters who were schoolgirls. One of these ladies might have a daughter going in the convent to be a nun. What a job that must have been for those mothers. They had the worry and concern as to whether the girl was doing the right thing, thinking of the loneliness of being without her, but also had to get a big trunk of clothes ready for her to take. The list would be sent from the Mother House of whatever order she was joining. The list would be something like: six nightdresses, much the same in each garment of underwear, one dozen pairs of long black hand-knitted stockings, black shoes and lots of other things. I remember one mother who had one of her eldest girls going to be a nun. She was a very busy farmer's wife with more young children, so grandmother knitted all the long black stockings for her. Grandmother was only too pleased to do it, for that lady was always very thoughtful and good for coming to pay a visit to her when she had time. The stockings had to be made with very fine wool but in later years this all changed and everything could be bought in the city shops and stores.

It was very nice the way those country women visited each other. One very nice old lady would walk about half a mile to visit grandmother, always on a Sunday, late evening. When people said to her you are wonderful for your age, she always said, 'Ah well, I have been very lucky. I have my passage paid now. I am only waiting for the Captain's Letter.' I once asked grandmother why she said this. I was told that when poor people in Ireland first started going to America they would start by sending half a crown to the office of the shipping company in Cork, every week, until they had paid their full fare to America. Then they would get what was called 'the Captain's Letter' telling them what day they would sail but, she said, Mrs Tracey meant her captain was God and that she had been a good wife and mother though she had had her troubles, so she had well paid her passage to heaven. I always thought, what a wonderful end to life.

9

The Donkey and Cart

The donkey and cart was a godsend to mothers living in the country, although mother loved her bicycle when she was in a hurry to get somewhere on her own. However, if Uncle Jim's pony and trap or dad's horse that was kept mostly for his post-office job were not handy, the donkey and cart was a wonderful way of taking small children to town or to visit family, school or even the doctor's. Men or women getting old in the country were never housebound if they had a donkey and cart. Mary, Peg and I were taken lots of places this way; of course, it would be only a few miles away from home. That did not matter, the thing was that as soon as we were told that we were going to be taken somewhere it was very exciting. I remember Mary being put to sleep and dad looking after her one time and mother telling me that we were going in the donkey and cart down to the hill of Kilmallock to visit Mr and Mrs Downs and their daughter May. They had only lately got a wireless. On the way there mother explained it all to me. I found it hard to understand, but I was going to be up late and that was wonderful.

Well, when we arrived at the home of the Downs family I cannot remember where poor Neddie was taken, but we were put sitting down. They were all fussing about the new invention perched on a little table near the window. To me it looked like a brown polished wooden box with a little window and knobs at the front. May was telling her father all about these little knobs, then a loud man's voice came out and everyone sat still. I felt they had nailed me to the dark straight chair they had put me sitting on. Another sign from mother of fingers on lips and then the man's voice they had been waiting for. It was the king of England telling his people that he was giving up his throne for the woman he loved. When he had finished speaking we had nice cake and I was given that lovely red O'Sullivan's lemonade as well. The adults had the best china teaset for their tea but May and my mother were in tears for the king and were cross with Mrs Simpson, the lady he had fallen in love with. The only pictures of kings I had seen were in my story books and I pictured him sitting there with a big crown and wearing a big cloak talking into a long tube that reached all the way from England to Downs' wireless. That was the first wireless I had seen and I did not think much of it. It was not as good as the gramophone Auntie Kit and Uncle Maurice had. So that would be 1936, the Abdication of Edward.

The donkey and cart had many uses. Someone with only two cows took his barrel of milk to the creamery that way and through the war many a bag of turf was settled up on the back of the donkey and cart, for some old lady, by one of the men that worked at the big coal and turf yard owned by Sutton's in Kilmallock.

I remember one very pretty girl from Bulgaden who had been nursing in London, bringing home a very nice young man for a holiday. I think he had been injured while at war because he looked very thin and pale and had a walking stick. She took him everywhere in the donkey and cart. They went shopping,

64

went to visit friends and family and to a few parties. He grew to love that way of travelling and said it did him the world of good.

The donkey and cart was often the first form of transport for a new baby. It was very safe and so steady. The mother could sit on her driving seat with little baby in a little basket-like, small cot, on the floor near her and the rocking would send baby to sleep. Small children would be put sitting on a long flat canvas cushion on the floor of the cart and in cold weather their feet and up to their waist would be covered in a warm rug and the children grew to love that donkey. Some people would keep them in the field all day, other people after they had fed them would let them graze along the roadside and with so few cars on the road, it was very safe for them. They would never move very far from their own homes. Sometimes when we were coming from school we would take a short ride on a donkey's back, but when mother found out I had done this she was very cross and said it was not very ladylike and that I may as well give up school and home and join the tinkers. She said that she would have to go and have a word with my teacher and that Miss Carroll would be shocked. I begged for mercy and promised never to do it again. She said, 'Well, if I ever hear you have broken your promise...' but I never did break my promise; mother always had a way of finding out everything, in our eyes.

10

My Visit to Stookeens

Auntie Hannie and Uncle Will, grandmother's sister and brother, often came to visit us at the bridge. Neither of them had ever married and after their parents had died they still lived at the old family home, Stookeens, a lovely old cottage a couple of miles up the road in Martinstown.

I am not sure what Uncle Will's job was, but he had worked at Mount Coote for Lord and Lady Greenall, so Auntie Hannie kept house for him. I heard in later years that when she was a young girl, men were brought in the hope of matching her for a husband, but that she was so very hard to please, no match was every made. I think Nell, Doris and I were a bit afraid of her when we were taken up there, for although she was nice to us and always had lovely nice surprise eats for tea, she would take no nonsense from children or from anyone else. When grandmother, Auntie Kit or mother asked her about some local girl that had married and moved away over the years, she would stand with maybe a fancy teapot to think for a second about the girl, then she would say, 'I know who you mean. Ah sure she is like the rest of you, a house full of bold children, God help her.'

Everything in the house, from the great big dresser in the kitchen with all sorts of willow-pattern dishes and plates, china pictures on the wall and the grandmother clock, were all in that house since their parents first came in there as a young couple and the house is still the same today. I remember one special fireside chair, Auntie Hannie telling me to sit up straight on. Of course, I did as I was told, she then smiled and said, 'That was your great-grandfather's fireside chair.' Now our children have sat on that chair and been told the story of how he enjoyed relaxing there, smoking his pipe. Soon after that Auntie Hannie took ill with a bad stroke and one of her nieces, who was her godchild, Peggy Coughlain, and lived out in Fermoy in County Cork, training to be a nanny, was visited by her father, Uncle Garrett, telling her that her godmother was ill and it was her job to go and help to nurse her. That was the end of Peggy's training for the post. She was looking forward to being like her sister who was now looking after some lord's children in Cork.

We as children were too young for some years to understand all that, so now going with mother and Auntie Kit and sometimes grandmother to help care for Auntie Hannie, I grew to be very fond of Peggy. She was the first person I heard call grandmother Aunt Kate. She had lovely sandy-coloured hair which she wore in a page boy style. Grandmother thought a lot of her, and often said how wonderfully she nursed Auntie Hannie and always kept her looking so nice in pink or blue or white nightdresses and matching lacy bed jackets. Mother and grandmother liked to try and help and Auntie Kit when she could but it was Peggy who spent all the long hours, as well as looking after Uncle Will.

Every so often they arranged that she should have some time off to go home to visit her parents, Uncle Garrett and Auntie Mary. Peggy would cycle from Martinstown all the way to Fermoy and I remember when she came back she always brought me sweets or nice biscuits. I think it was mother and dad that would call to Stookeens some Sunday evenings to let Peggy come down to us to the bridge, for a break. She would always bring a nice cake for tea and she was a beautiful singer and would sing songs that grandmother liked.

Then Auntie Hannie died and there was a very big funeral. I remember lots of relations coming, lots that my cousins and I did not know. Sarsfield people from County Cork, because our great-grandmother's name was Kathleen Sarsfield, a descendant of Patrick Sarsfield. I heard later that she had always said that her wake was not to have too much drink flowing. A drop of whiskey for the respectable men and a drop of sherry for the ladies, so how they were expected to know which men were the respectable men I don't know, but I am sure poor Uncle Will and the rest of the family made sure that they did not do anything to displease her wishes.

I am not sure how long Auntie Hannie's illness went on but I am sure it was now too late for Peggy to return to her training to be a nanny. I expect Uncle Will was now getting older, because in those days men did not retire in the country jobs, so to me he seemed to go to work for a long time after. So Peggy stayed on looking after him. We now saw her very often and I am sure she was able to visit family and friends more and her sister would come for a holiday. I was so excited one Sunday when Peggy had been for a visit to grandmother's and she told me that they all had wondered if I would like to go in a few days for a holiday with her at Stookeens. Well, of course, I jumped for joy. Little did I know while I was playing out this wonderful idea had come up.

Well, we all said goodbye to Peggy for that evening and then I had to find out what day I would be going to Stookeens on my very own. I asked grandmother if I could have a small suitcase that was in her bedroom. She said yes, I could have it but that I must take good care of it, for she had had it a long time. She told me mother would tell me what clothes I was to take and sure enough the following day mother arrived with my holiday clothes all ready. They were put on a chair and both of us went through them. There were a few summer dresses, a warm skirt and jumper, which I put up a fight not to take, but was told that if there was any more nonsense I would not be going at all, so I thought I'd better be quiet and take the awful wintry-looking things. Then there was my best nightdress and a selection of underwear, my best Sunday shoes, blazer and hat, sandals and socks. Ribbons, handkerchiefs and that was it. I was told Peggy would have any other things I would need. The hated hairbrush was put in and I had to give mother a demonstration for her and grandmother of how well I could brush my hair. All the warnings I got, to be very good and helpful for Peggy, to be very polite when eating at the table, to speak up when Uncle Will or anyone that came to Stookeens spoke to me.

Well, it was not easy to get off to sleep that night but morning arrived. I ran as usual in my nightdress down the stairs to grandmother's downstairs bedroom and perched myself on her bed. I was now able to help her to wash and dress and we would say our morning prayers. Grandmother had a lot of prayers to say and would be still on her knees while I went in the kitchen and started to get our breakfast ready, the way mother had shown me. Some of the hens would now have laid their eggs and a lot of clucking and crowing would be coming from the little stoned yard and wall that made a square around the hen house. Uncle Jim would have fed them all with hot grain mash before he went to work, also the pig, for whom I always had a good morning and a few pats between his big ears.

A call of 'Bet, Bet,' from grandmother and I knew it was time to go to her and help her up off her knees. We had every little move and turn well worked out, so it became a very easy routine for us.

That particular morning I could not wait to get breakfast over. I found my little case that I had, I suppose, driven everyone mad with for the past couple of days. My ribbons, socks, some underwear and handkerchiefs were in it, but my other clothes had disappeared. Grandmother told me that they would not fit in my little case and anyway it would have been too much for me to carry and that Uncle Jim had taken them to Stookeens after I had gone to bed the night before. At first I was not too pleased to hear this. It was a bit of an intrusion into my holiday plans, but when I again opened the case and had another look at the things inside, I realised I would never have been able to take them all, so it was very kind of Uncle Jim to help me out.

Well, I was dressed ready. Grandmother had let me put on my favourite summer dress. I got down on my knees in front of her while she did my hair and put a nice bow at the back. I loved wearing my socks and sandals, I could run great in those, up and down ditches! I wore my blazer, my straw hat perched on my head, suitcase in one hand and my mother doll on my other arm. Said goodbye to grandmother and off I went. I knew the way very well. On passing Mollie Brazil's, I stopped at the gate to tell her I was now off to Stookeens for my holidays. She told me to have a lovely time, give her love to Peggy and how she would be counting the days until I would be coming back with lots to tell her and promised how she would visit grandmother when any of the family were not with her. I then headed off over the road for about two hundred yards until I came to Dewires Cross. I turned right there past Dewires cottage, also Mollie's brother's house and then the trees met overhead. This was a very quiet road. I soon came in sight of Culls, a great big house surrounded in trees, just a glimpse of the cream walls of the house appeared through the trees. Just a short distance down the road and on the other side was another great big house, Crowley's. A grey house and not much of this house could be seen from the road, just lots of great big trees. A lot of crows made their homes in these trees and they were the only company for me and my mother doll, but we were soon out in the light and were at Martinstown Cross. Mr and Mrs Flanningan's beautiful bungalow with its lovely garden stood out and the whole place looked lovely, bright and sunny. I then turned to the left, down past Cassey's cottage. I was now getting very excited because I only had to pass another Crowley's farmhouse and that was always full of life around it. A big, busy farmyard and when one of their dogs barked Miss Brigid would always come out. I liked her, she was a good friend of Peggy's. Well, that day the dogs did bark and Miss Brigid did come out. She knew all about I going to have a holiday with Peggy and Uncle Will, and said Peggy and I would be coming down to have tea with her one afternoon. I was now very near the end of my journey. I said goodbye to Miss Brigid and was just starting off when Peggy came down the road to meet me.

There was a big hug, she took my case and took off my hat, the cottage door was open like all houses in the country, so we were soon in and sitting down talking our heads off. Peggy was great for having O'Sullivan's lemonade in the parlour, and I so enjoyed it after the walk from the bridge. She always had a tin of Kerry Cream biscuits and also coconut biscuits. I called them 'fluffy ones', because I could not remember their names. After a rest we went upstairs to put my clothes away in Peggy's bedroom. I was so pleased when she told me I could sleep with her in the great big bed that belonged to grandmother's parents. A new mattress was made every so often for that bed. Peggy let me climb on to the bed and jump and bounce on it. Everything in that bedroom was very old and on the wall not far from the bed was the big grandmother clock that had been a wedding gift to my great-grandparents. A man from Cork called every so often to check and clean it. I loved this old house because I had heard so many stories about it from grandmother. Peggy and Uncle Will did not have a pig, hens or any animals, only a cat, a lovely Persian cat, a very proud-looking cat I always thought. He was tall and had a dark, browny grey, silk coat. His name was Teskin Tooks and he had a special cushion of his own up on the deep window ledge, where he liked to sun himself every morning.

Peggy asked me the first morning if I would like to stay in bed for a while. She had to get up early to get Uncle Will's breakfast. I told her I would love to get up and have breakfast with him, so she said I could. I always loved a good cooked breakfast, so for the week getting up about 6 a.m. and sitting up at the table with my great-uncle and having a good chat and a great tuck in was a wonderful start to the day. Peggy would be busy getting a lunch pack ready for him. I got to know him so well that week. He told me stories of when grandmother and himself and their brothers and sisters were young and what school was like. They did not have exercise books or jotters, they had slates and chalk to write on. He would give a quick look at the big watch that he kept in his waistcoat pocket and off out to tackle up his donkey and cart. He would drive round to the front of the house, where Peggy would have a canvas bag with his lunch inside. He would take this, wave us goodbye and off he would go to Mount Coote. I remember when he would come home at night, Peggy would have a big dinner ready. The table would always be set lovely. They would have chops, beef, chicken, meals like that, one night homecure, but Peggy cooked homecure for me most evenings. At this Uncle Will would laugh and say 'Your grandfather at the bridge will never be dead while you are alive!' He had them cook it at a hotel in Cork for him once. I often heard that story.

Peggy and I enjoyed our days together. Mamy Barry lived just up the road a bit from them and she had a country shop, so I would go for shopping. I liked Mamy, she was always nice and often gave me some conversation lozenges and she would let me put the bags of stuff on the weighing scales. Peggy and I helped her with her flower bed one afternoon and then she came down to have afternoon tea with us and brought a lovely cake and of course we had tea and O'Sullivan's lemonade with Brigid Crowley. Then one morning Uncle Will said he would leave us the donkey and cart so we could have a day out in Kilfinnane and that meant he had a long walk to work, but he did not mind.

I enjoyed Kilfinnane. I had heard from grandmother the names of the shops that were also there when she was a girl. We had a wonderful day out, did all the shopping and got a chunk of tobacco for Uncle Will, St Bruno's. We went in the beautiful church that stands up the hill near the convent, said a prayer, came out and met a lovely little old lady with her shawl wrapped round her. Peggy told her who I was. She told me she knew grandmother and remembered her mother. She made us come in for tea. She had a lovely little parlour and took out lovely cups and saucers. I was worried to death in case I would drop one of them, but I am glad to say, I didn't. Unlike the girl at school she told me I had the Sarsfields' red hair and that it only came out every so often in families. She sent her love to grandmother and Uncle Will. We thanked her and set off on

74

our journey home. That was Saturday, so next day, Sunday, I went with Peggy walking to Martinstown Church to mass. There was a shop near there, I cannot remember the name, but I had a penny and Peggy let me spend it. I got some few sweets, which I saved as take-home gifts.

Next day, Monday, I had a big surprise, Auntie Kit, Auntie Peg and a gentleman in a grey suit arrived. I did not know Auntie Peg was home. Why was I not told? I knew mother and Uncle Jim had been painting and wallpapering and they said it would all be lovely when I would get back from my holiday, but it did not mean much. I had seen all that sort of thing before, but when the three of them came in to Peggy's parlour, Auntie Peg hugged me and told me to shake hands with Uncle Sam. He told me he had heard all about me and how good I was for grandmother. I liked him from the very start. He started looking in different pockets of a mackintosh for sweets and money and found some in those deep pockets. I was having a wonderful time. Uncle Will came early from work, another secret kept from me. The big parlour was all set for a lovely meal, roast chicken and all the trimmings. Uncle Sam was told lots of stories of Stookeens. Well, it was time for them to go. They told me they would see me next day when I would go home to grandmother's. It was soon time for me to go to bed. My mind kept straying over my prayers. I had a lot to think about after the day. Peggy and I were up early as usual and I had breakfast with Uncle Will. We talked about my new Uncle Sam and he said, 'Isn't it nice having a new uncle and I think he is a very nice man.' I agreed with him. He then went to his bookshelf and came across with a brown paper bag and gave it to me. When I opened it I could see a lovely pencil case with all the special bits and best of all a grand rubber. He also gave me a shilling and said he would tell mother what a good girl I had been. I thanked him and gave him a hug. He got up on the donkey and cart and I waved until he went around the bend of the road.

Later in the day dad came for me and took me to grand-mother's where there was a big family reunion. That night sitting with mother on grandmother's bed, I told them both how much I liked our new uncle. Grandmother said she was so happy for Auntie Peg that she was not alone in England any more and that we would be expecting them both home from now on.

11

The War Years

I was ten years old when the Second World War broke out and with still only very few people having a wireless, on that September morning, the word got around the countryside by word of mouth from one person to another. It was all very upsetting because some families had sons who had joined the army or air force in England and then there were lots of sons and daughters who were priests, nuns, nurses, missionaries in other countries.

My mother's young first cousin Lena Coughlain, who had gone to France to the Mother House of the Little Sisters of the Poor, had only just finished her first year as a postulant in the convent near Paris. I remember her mother, who had another daughter, a nun, in England, coming to see grandmother. Then there was another cousin of mother's, a nurse just finishing her training at a hospital in Liverpool and dad's three sisters, one in Birmingham, one in Bristol and I think the other in one of the large London hospitals. As children we all became very familiar with the names 'Hitler', 'Chamberlain' and for many years 'Mr Churchill', and we could pick up from bits we heard being read out of newspapers by adults all about how awful the bombing was in such and such a city in England. Letters from overseas were taking much longer to come and they were now censored, so I suppose it took a long time opening up all those letters and sealing them up again. At school we were taken to church more than ever to pray for peace. Mrs O'Brien would point out on the great big maps that hung on the big classroom walls where very worrying parts of the war were taking place. At home, family prayers were all for peace and offering the rosary for someone's son that was out at the front. Poor grandmother now started saying an extra rosary. I remember when she would have finished, she would make the sign of the cross and say 'God help the mothers of the world.'

Now I was more grown up and able to help grandmother more and let mother look after the family in Ballingaddy, but mother and Auntie Kit came to the bridge a lot, also dad, Uncle Maurice, Uncle Bill and Uncle Pad. Auntie Mary was not able to come so much. Uncle Jim would be busy, after working different hours wherever he could get work. There was rationing of such things as tea, sugar, butter, clothes and paraffin oil, which was our only means of light in those days. Candles became a very rare sight and so did very many other everyday things that were needed. Ireland was an island and we kept being told that there were no ships or boats to bring all these very important things we were in need of.

Coal seemed to disappear and in our homes and at school it was turf fires. We got an extra week's holiday in the summer to help parents saving the turf on the mountain. I did not help on the mountain much. Mary, Peg and I would stay with grandmother, but after dad's post round in the morning he and mother would go up to Blackrock mountain and work hard, he having to cut and dig out the big, damp slabs of turf. They had to be spread out to dry and next day made into little piles. The next day he would have the 'horse and rail' down near the lower part of the mountain and they had two wheelbarrows. While dad took one full of turf down to the rail, mother would be filling up the other because he had to come home in the evening in time for his post round again. Mother, although a small woman, would wheel a barrow down herself just to hurry things up.

The few times I went with them I enjoyed it very much. Mary and I picked up all the small bits of turf and put them in bags. The picnic lunch was great, of course, the thing was it was all so different from our everyday jobs at home. I cannot remember how long all this work took because dad could not put in very long hours like others did, but then lots of them had to come down home to milk cows and do other farm jobs. I think dad sometimes hired a big rail to bring the turf home quicker. A great big rick would be set up at the back of the house. Uncle Jim helped when he could, often on a Sunday, when the priest said from the altar, 'God will understand it's a fine day and we must keep the home fire and the school fire going for the winter, so we had all better get up that mountain after second mass today.'

A lot of turf was always taken to grandmother's and grand-father, at Ballingaddy and, with a lot of woods not far away, dad, Uncle Jim, Larry Brazil and Mick Neville would buy a very big tree. This was a big job to take on. Larry was the best climber, he would head up to the top of the great big tree and settle a big strong rope on it. He would be calling down instructions to the three men below. Then the cutting had to start and, with no electric saws at that time, two of them would start off with a great long saw with a handle on each end. They would work hard at this for a long time and with still a lot of the great big trunk to get through they would take a break while the two others took over and on it went until the great monster fell to the ground. They would also have wedges and hatchets and smaller saws. It would all have to be cut down into small blocks of wood, divided up and brought home and when you think – these jobs were done in their so-called spare time. Neither the school nor any old people ever went without a fire. I remember children picking 'kippins' (little pieces of dried up wood), on their way to school, to help the teacher to light the fire but, because this made them a little late, she tried to say she would light the fire without any help.

By now I was able to go to places like Kilmallock, for grandmother, on my own. Mother kept my ration book at grandmother's and that was now one of my weekly jobs. But I grew to dislike it so much, because every evening of the week, after school, at one time, I walked in the snow and frost in the Bulgaden road to Kilmallock to find out the rations had not come to the shop and I had the sad walk back to tell grand-mother. Dad and mother and lots of other people did not always get those weekly rations. The word got around that they had been stolen out of the goods train for the Black Market. How we hated those words. Dad, mother and the rest of us often had to drink Camp coffee without sugar, or milk, hot sometimes, cold others. We would try to save the bit of tea and sugar when we got it for grandmother, because she was now getting older and did not take a lot of food. I remember she enjoyed scrambled egg on little pieces of toast. I was so pleased when she said I done it so nice.

Meat, eggs, milk, apples, blackberries, strawberries and vege-tables we had plenty of, but we had no sugar for cooking and the lovely light, white flour disappeared. The bag of flour that came at home in Ballingaddy was a dark brown, nearly black and it did not taste very nice. Mothers kept a bit of white muslin made into a little bag. They would fill it with the awful flour and keep shaking it for ages into a baking pan, until they got a little bit of the white flour out of it. This was made into a little cake for someone in the family that was ill and not eating very much, but thank God the good old homecure bacon still stayed with us.

I remember an old man that often passed our house in Ballingaddy in his donkey and cart. He would be on his way home from Kilmallock. His wife was long dead and I think it used to get him down, the idea of the rations. The half gallon of paraffin oil did not last him long. He still had his little vegetable garden. Mother would ask one of us to tell her when he was coming near the house. She would run out to him with a nice bit of homecure. His face would light up, 'God bless you missus, that now with my spuds and grand bit of cabbage and a bit of mustard, sure a man would attack Hitler with the bare knuckles!' We would say to mother, 'Old Tom is very brave.' Sometimes, if someone was passing his house on a horse and trap and mother had a fine dinner keeping warm for him, she would wrap cloths round the two plates and send Mary and I off with his dinner. We never told whoever had given us the lift what we were taking to him. I remember often sitting on one of those traps and feeling the dinner a bit too hot on my knees. Mary would always run and knock at his door. He would open it and say, 'Run and put it on the table. God Bless yer mother and ye are not bad girls either!' Sometimes he would have a bottle of lemonade. He would pour it out in cups for us. He would get a knife and fork from a drawer, sit down, unwrap the dinner, take his hat off and rest it on one of his knees, make the sign of the cross and say 'Glory be to God on High, only for the bit we eat we would die!' He would give a look up and say 'Thank you God.' That was usually Sunday dinner. For a while he was very cross because someone's goat was coming into his garden and eating his cabbage. He kept asking us if we knew whose goat was on the loose, but like him we were not sure. We went through all the people we knew that had a goat, but they all had a fetter on and could not climb ditches. He sat back in the chair one day and said, 'Girls, it will not be known whose goat had my cabbage until the day of the Reveille.' That was what he always called the day of Last Judgement. I remember Mary and I walking home and Mary saying 'As if God will bring up that day what goat ate his cabbage.' We both agreed that God would have far too much to think of that day.

Farmers too were pretty fed up with a man that came around from the government every so often in the springtime. He was called the 'tillage inspector' and would tell farmers how much land should be ploughed up to grow crops on. They were already fed up not being able to get parts for their farm machinery and sometimes he was a bit too much for them. I was very proud of Uncle Maurice one day when he was showing this man how well he had followed the rules. The tillage inspector, all dressed up in a smart suit, walked so carefully into a difficult bit of ground by a ditch and said to Uncle Maurice, 'I am sure if you tried you could get the horse and plough in here?' At this he was soon told, 'If you do not get off my land I will run the plough up your arse!'

Another upsetting thing for farmers was that they supplied milk to the local creamery, but butter was rationed so, to make up for the loss, we were given a ration of Red Rose margarine. It was not nice to taste, a big, hard block; I found dry bread better, but thank God, people were still able to have our wonderful homecure bacon. I would have exchanged all my very poor rations for that, including my sweet ration and I sincerely hope the Common Market bureaucrats do not stumble across it one day in their paperwork and decide to destroy the

82

feeding habit of the wonderful Irish pig, that gives us the wonderful bacon.

Clothes, boots and shoes caused a lot of worry for mothers. Shoes were mended as much as they possibly could be. Old jumpers and cardigans were given where there were young children and they were unpicked. Mother showed me how to unpick something hand knitted, at its seams, so carefully and then how to unwind. This was made in to long hanks, washed and dried out in the open air to take the marks of the knitting stitches out if it; then when dry, someone would hold it on two outstretched hands, like a frame, while someone else rolled it up in a ball. Bits of wool would be mixed and matched, not a scrap would be wasted.

I remember Grandfather Ballingaddy was a very big man and always wore navy, serge suits. When the knees were showing wear, he would give them to mother. She would boil ivy leaves in a big pot for ages, then strain off all the water. She would have unpicked all the seams and stitching of the trousers, then all the pieces would be washed by hand in the water and pressed damp. The material would look like new when the worn bits were cut out. I remember she made gym slips for school out of these. Flour bags were boiled until they were snow white. The big bags she could get a little blouse out of but nightdresses were often made out of the front of the sack, that often had a faint '28lbs' written across. Auntie Mary once gave her a coat that was starting to fade on the shoulders. Mother unpicked it all and turning out the wrong side of the material made me a lovely best coat. Nothing was wasted. People would be telling each other of some wonderful idea they had come up with to make do.

All men in those days smoked, whether pipes or cigarettes and they were not rationed but were very hard to get. The word would get around that some country shop or a town, a fair distance away, had got 'smokes' and off you would see go some man in a hurry on horseback, or an old rusty bicycle. I remember once a lady asking me if my grandmother was okay. I said yes. She said, 'Thank God. The way I saw your Uncle Jim rushing on the horse I thought he was going for the priest for her, but my husband said, "There are fags at Higgins's, I bet that is what he is rushing for!"'

It was getting difficult to keep bicycles on the road in good repair. Tyres and tubes were hard to come by and on rough country roads they did not last long. Auntie Peg had been home on a holiday and had bought me a fine second-hand bicycle. It was wonderful to travel from home to grandmother's, over to Auntie Kit's and Auntie Mary's at Ballyhea, about one mile from Ballingaddy church and up to Stookeens in Martinstown. That same bike was handed on down the generations and I think one or two of them started their courting days on it.

I would take them all the local news and bring back all their news, but my tyres and tubes began to wear out and poor dad had to go to the Black Market for tyres. He was charged one pound each, which was a great lot of money then. A few weeks had to pass in between him getting both of them. I remember Uncle Jim finding some way of getting tubes; I think he done some work for someone to cover the cost. It was the first example of people who had such a love for money over their belief in principles. Whatever was scarce or on ration these people knew ways of getting a stock tucked away and knew how to circle it about in a quiet way from the law. So when it was suggested to me that from now on I would be better saving my bicycle for only very important journeys, I was only too pleased to go along with it.

12

My Visits to Knocklong

Lots of people walked miles in those days. I remember sometimes grandmother being up with us at Ballingaddy and if it
happened that our homecure had run out, because we could
only afford to kill one pig, mother might have a great big chicken
roasted or some stew or whatever, so after a few days of this and
knowing grandmother was okay and happy with the family, I
would hit off on foot to Knocklong for my good dinner of
homecure.

I knew Uncle Maurice had four pigs killed in the year. I was
often allowed to put on my very best clothes. I would say
goodbye to them all and start my journey off down the road,
past Lynch's, Dolan's, Quinn's and then up the big hill. I would
turn back and look at our house down the hill from me; they
were all usually out at the side of the house waving to me. I
would wave back, continue off down the road around the bend.
The beautiful church of Ballingaddy would be there in front of
me. I would go in it, kneel at the back, say a quick prayer, give a
few skips out the gate and down the road to Hockinson's Cross.

This now was the start of a lovely walk. Riversfield Road just
had a cottage dotted here and there. The great house of Mount
Coote was on my left-hand side and Riversfield House on my

right-hand side. Hopping up and down ditches and walls I could hear the lovely hum that was like soft music from the telegraph wires that ran through the trees. How is it there was no danger for children then? The people I would meet were usually on horseback, maybe the odd donkey and cart. I would carry on down to Leahy's Cross, a lovely big farmhouse on the right. Their big grey and white cat was always spread out on the wall. At that time I was sure that cats looked very like whatever their owners looked like. Leahy's cat most certainly did look a farmer and the big smoky grey cat with big eyes that sat on the convent wall was a reverend mother. Those big eyes looked you up and down. The cat that always sat on one of the high piers of the parish priest's gate was long and quite slim, black with just a few patches of white and looked down on us and gave a few sharp meows. He was bound to be a priest in the pulpit. I would then turn left onto the main road up hill and down hollow until I would get to Ballinscaula Bridge. I would have a quick chat with Mrs Neville. Grandmother's house would be shut up for the day, but Mollie and Larry would treat me as a visitor although I had only been in there the day before. I was given a drink of tea or lemonade if Mollie was able to get it. It was nice and lovely to have been made a fuss of, but I would now have to hurry off on the rest of my journey to be there when Auntie Kit was dishing up dinner.

When I got to Elton village about a mile or so from the bridge I knew I did not have far to go. It was on to the little by-road near John Creed's, that big hardware/grocer's shop in Elton. I would walk along until I saw Major Webb's on the right-hand side from the next crossroad, then I would turn to the left for about half a mile to near Brown's shop and then I could see Auntie Kit and Uncle Maurice's fine, big Georgian farmhouse. Sometimes my cousins would be playing out near the great big gates and they would run back up the road to meet me, saying, 'Have you come for dinner? We were expecting you!' In I would go with them. There would be a big hug from Auntie Kit. Uncle Maurice and the two workmen would be on their way in from the fields or the barn or someplace. Mary Halloran was a woman that for years helped Auntie Kit with the housework and looking after the family. Two tables were set for dinner in the great big kitchen. Uncle Maurice sat at the head of the table; Auntie Kit would be busy seeing that the little ones, Jim and Hanna May, were eating. Poor Moss may have been getting up to a bit of mischief. Tom was always very gentle. Nell now looked very grown up to me and would be putting Moss in his place. Doris and I always had a bit of fun going between us. About four of us would sit on a long seat/stool on the inside of the big table. I often sat next to Uncle Maurice. He always said what a great girl I was for coming all that way to have my dinner with them and that some people sitting around the table were hopeless eaters. I think he was making an example of me to encourage the little ones to eat, and how I enjoyed those beautiful dinners and a great afternoon of fun and play with my cousins.

Both Nell and Doris played the piano beautifully. It was so wonderful to sit in the great big parlour that had all the black furniture with blue and gold round the pictures to mark out various corners. There was a little picture of Marie Antoinette, the last queen of France, on one piece of furniture and there was the great big round table with the one big leg that came into three little claw legs as it stood proudly in the centre of the parlour. In summer Auntie Kit always had a lovely bunch of sweetpeas in the centre of that table. The parlour had two very big windows that seemed to reach from ceiling to floor.

Then the visit was over and I was ready for home. If the

horse that went under the trap was not busy doing other work, I would have been taken home but, of course, in the spring and other times that the farm was busy this was not possible, so I would set off walking. Auntie Kit and Uncle Maurice would both agree if school was opening up in a few days, that I should be given a good piece of homecure to take home and they were so good, for they always gave me some of their tea and sugar ration for grandmother. Everything would have been put in a bag and I would guard this well on my way home. Sometimes I would get a lift from someone with a donkey and cart or horse and cart. As children we met people we knew on all these roads that would give us a lift. So when they asked me had I been to see my auntie and her family, I would only be too pleased to pour out all about the wonderful visit to Knocklong.

13

The War Years Continued

Well, the dreadful war still shadowed our childhood for some years and the sight of a telegram boy on his big, post office bicycle became such a cause of worry to so many people. When he called to someone's house and handed a small brown envelope to whoever came to the door and who took it from him, their hands would tremble as they opened it and took out the square of white paper with the black strips of print telling the very brief message. It might say that a son who was at war had been killed or was missing or known to be seriously wounded and, with a lot of families having sons as priests or missionaries and daughters as nuns, all in war-torn countries, very often sad news came of what had happened to them also. Mother's lovely young cousin Lena Coughlain who had not yet been professed in the order of The Little Sisters of the Poor, was reported missing. The only news that reached home was that the enemy forces had occupied Paris and the convent was set on fire around the nuns and orphaned children. Lena's father had died some years before, but her poor mother and the rest of the family were heartbroken. Her mother would sit with grand-mother trying to picture what must have happened. She would say she must keep going for the rest of her children, but the poor woman worried and wondered what happened to her Lena until the day she died. Of course, news often also came of deaths or injuries of people who were working in England. I think it was mostly of girls nursing in the big cities.

So, we were often taken from school back to Bulgaden church for special masses and prayers. I think when we stood at the end of mass and sang 'Faith of Our Fathers,' we really did take in what the words were all about, now that we were hearing so much of how people were suffering for their faith, especially Jewish people. There were lots of prayers and rosaries said for peace and of course we knew even as children that if England was invaded we would not stand much chance, but thank God it never came to that.

Poor Mrs Neville, who was praying for peace, had died. She had not long been on bed rest and when Mick, her son, had to go somewhere of an evening I would go and sit by her bed, settle her pillows and give her a drink. Mollie Brazil came in one evening and when I told her Mrs Neville was talking to people that were not there, I remember Mollie sitting on the bed holding one of her hands and saying, there is nothing we can do. Mick came back and was sad to see the big change in his mother. I remember he went straight off to Kilmallock for the doctor and I think it was one of the young men of the Cleary's that went off down to Bulgaden for the priest, who arrived first. By now someone had helped grandmother out to Neville's and she was sitting by the bedside, sponging Mrs Neville's face with a cool cloth that she dipped in and out of a bowl of water. Doctor Ogilvie's new, big, blue motorcar pulled up at the gate. He came in and went straight to poor Mrs Neville. On his way out he told Mick that her heartbeat was nearly gone and how sorry he was to see her slipping away. He, like a lot of people loved to have a chat with her. He was a lovely man and had been a British Army Doctor in the First World War and came to live with his nice wife in Kilmallock. Well, in the early hours of the next morning Mrs Neville died. When I got up at grandmother's I was told to get dressed in my best dress and hair ribbons and told to go to Mrs Neville's bedside and have a last goodbye and say a prayer for her. By now all the family were there; the house was full of people. I felt very strange, but one of her daughters-in-law came to the door to me and took me to her bedroom where she was now all laid out in her brown habit and all the lovely lace linen and lace bedding all round her. I remember giving her a kiss on the cheek and she was so cold. I was then taken out to the kitchen. Lots of people were arriving for the wake. There was lots to eat and drink and Auntie Kit and Auntie Mary arrived. I remember sitting near mother and looking around at pictures and orna-ments that she had often told me stories about and, without thinking, I said, 'What will happen to her lovely tin of biscuits now?' Mother gave me a look that nearly nailed me to the floor. I felt so sorry and felt the tears blinding my eyes for I loved Mrs Neville, but I was soon cheered up hearing funny stories about her.

One lady with a big feather in her hat and drinking from a small glass said, 'God rest her soul. You know once she told me it was more rewarding giving a good dinner to a pig than to an ill-mannered man! For the pig when he had eaten his dinner would give you a pleasing grunt, but the ill-mannered man when he had eaten his dinner would just push his plate away from him without a word.'

Someone else said, if you told her about someone who had come up in the world and was not a very considerate boss to work for, she would say, 'Well, if you put a beggar on horseback he will ride to hell,' or 'It is not always good for a country to have dung hills rising and castles falling!' and so the stories about her went on.

She was taken into church that evening and buried next day with her husband in Athneasy. I was taken to the church, to Bulgaden, the night she was laid in her coffin in front of the altar where she had been baptised as a baby. The next day of her funeral I was at school but when I got home in the evening I missed her a lot. It was another very special, good friend gone out of my life, but time went on and more sad news from the war.

More people were getting a wireless and they would ask neighbours in to hear the BBC news. I remember Mollie and Larry got one. Mollie would put it on for me if there was nice singing or a good ceilidh band on which was wonderful. It brought the house alive. Mollie and I would line up to dance a reel or a jig. We did not have much of the hornpipe, but we had a good laugh and could not believe just to turn a little black knob all the wonder that was now coming into Mollie's kitchen. It was lovely too hearing John McCormack and on Sunday evenings for a while grandmother allowed me to go over to Mollie to hear Barbara Mullins singing. She always finished with her usual song:

> I'm a rambler, I'm a gambler,
> I'm a long way from home,
> If you don't like me,
> Then leave me alone.
>
> I eat when I'm hungry,
> I drink when I'm dry,
> And if moonshine don't kill me,
> I will live till I die.

Larry would always join in at the last line, 'And if the black bread don't kill us we will live till we die!' Mollie then always said to him, 'There are worse off than you in this war.'

Grandmother always told me to come home the minute Barbara had finished because people would be going in to hear the news. Although Mollie and Larry often asked grandmother if she would like to come and hear the wireless, she always thanked them for their kind offer, but never did go. I am sure being confined to two walking sticks had a lot to do with it, but she did discuss it with people who would visit and I remember hearing her say, 'What a wonderful age we live in. To think that people can sit by their own fireside and hear the voice of someone from Dublin and even London give them so much news of what is going on. Why do we have to have this awful war spoiling all these wonderful inventions?' However, grand-mother enjoyed the newspapers and thought they had gone a long way and so did mother and dad for that matter. The *Limerick Leader* was the paper Uncle Jim got mostly. Both grandmother and himself would be commenting on it. I remember at one stage being fascinated by the auctions of great big houses and their contents: every little detail of all of someone's possessions would be so well described down to the smallest things. Also farms that were up for auction, all the house contents, down to buckets, pots, pans, sets of china. It was unbelievable and I always wondered how long it took whoever made out those long lists. Then they would go outside, barns, outhouse contents, farm machinery. I always wished I had lots of money and was grown up enough to go to one of those wonderful auctions.

The *Cork Examiner* was I think the weekly paper. I know that grandmother and I always looked forward to reading the weekly column by 'Rambling Tady', a reporter who travelled around the country chatting to the locals in some part of Cork, Kerry, Limerick, Tipperary and maybe other places. It was always very interesting and often very funny. He drew lots of people to that newspaper.

I think dad, like lots of men, picked the newspaper that was best for sport. Sunday morning after mass he loved that space in time from then to Sunday dinner, about one o'clock. He would sit there soaking it all up. He would be checking between the Limerick paper and the Irish press. He loved sport and of course Sunday was the only day men had for sport in those days. Sometimes it would have to be early dinner because if there was a hurling match a fair journey away, in order to see it, he and lots of those men had to go on their bicycles there. Only a short time before he died, when I went home to see him and mother, we got talking of those years and he told me that one Sunday he went on his bicycle to Thurles, about fifteen miles away, to watch some special hurling match. It was still wartime and the two inner tubes were not very good and there was no hope of getting new ones. He said he got seven punctures on the way. He had his little box of patches, so every so often it was the bicycle upside down and a quick repair. He said he enjoyed the match and his bicycle was kind to him on the way home. So he must have done a good job on it going. Mother sat listening to him and when he had finished she said, 'You could not wait for the report of the match to appear in the *Limerick Leader*. If your team won you were all smiles reading the report out loud, but if they lost, the paper had it all wrong!'

Of course, *Ireland's Own* came into all our homes in those days. We loved the short stories, some that would continue the next week, but I am sure it is 'Kitty the Hare' that stands out in most people's minds. Before you started the story and opening the page there was the picture of Kitty, wearing a great big,

94

black cloak with its hood up on her head and her story always started something like this: 'Come on now, let us gather around the fire, God bless us. Can you hear the howling wind banging the trees off the window panes. Well, it was on such a night in a lonely part of West Cork, I was winding my way down a road and suddenly there in front of me stood...' That was enough for me of one of those ghost stories. I would have to read on, but even in daylight she put fear in me.

The little red book, *The Messenger*, was a lovely little book to read. I think it was the first kind of teenage reading we had as well as having stories and bits of interest for adults. There were stories of young girls of our ages, some country girls, some city girls, being part of families or being an only child. Everything came over in a sensible way, no rosy pictures but a good attitude to life.

We also looked forward to our copy of *The Far East* but, because it was war years when we were growing up, books in the countryside seemed to be ones we had read before and we were just not very interested in the others. Mother always loved reading but in those war years with people only getting half a gallon of paraffin oil for the light, it was difficult. The winter evenings, with it being dark so early, meant after supper and homework was done and the children scrubbed and put to bed, the lamp had to be put out and adults sat around a blazing fire for the rest of the night.

14

The Railway

Ballinscaula railway bridge was always a place of interest for me as a child. I was well warned and well watched not to climb over the long, low wall that joined up with the big, high railway bridge at what we called 'our' side of the road. The low wall suited me fine, for I could stand near it and get a good view down on to the railway. The big, long, green grassy slopes that ran from a ditch down to the side of the railway track would look like a meadow in the summer. Every spring a gentleman from the railways would come and rent a section of these slopes for one shilling to anyone that would need the grass, or hay I should say. Uncle Jim, Mick Neville and Larry Brazil always rented some of it for bedding for animals. That was great, the only trouble was that in those days the engines of all the trains had a man stoking up a big, coal fire and when he had that engine fire at its best, it would send sparks of fire flying in the air and sometimes on a warm day they would land on one of those slopes and start a fire. So sometimes when they were expecting a goods train or one of the passenger trains to pass, it was my job to run up to the bridge and see if a fire was starting in one of the slopes after the train had passed. If it had, I would run for all I was worth to tell them, then I would watch from the wall as one or two of them would climb on to the slope with shovels and belt it hard until the fire went out. They usually took a bucket of water with them as well.

There was one time when on a Sunday, Cork may have beaten Limerick at Croke Park in Dublin at hurling. The special Cork trains taking the hurling team and all their supporters home would pass through County Limerick and their fireman would make sure they sent sparks flying high in the air as the trains came out of each railway bridge, but if Cork had lost they would be sitting very quiet in their seats and not let on to see the Limerick flag draped on each railway bridge. Of course, very few people in the county had a wireless and someone might have had to ride a bicycle down to Higgins's in Bulgaden to find out who won the match. Then they would have plenty of time to get ready for the Cork trains. It was all good fun. I remember at one time Mick Mackey was a great Limerick hurler, so his name was often called out.

Grandmother often told me about the grand opening of the Dublin-to-Cork railway. Her father and uncle were very pleased to get a job, something to do with the maintaining of the tracks, but she said everyone that lived anywhere near a railway bridge or station, the new in thing, was very excited on the day of the official opening. Queen Victoria came across to Dublin and rode on the first train on its way to Cork. To the people watching it went past Ballinscaula bridge very quickly. They just got a glimpse of a little lady in black who waved to them, but I often saw at grandmother's old home a fairly large framed photo of the queen being welcome by the lord mayor of Cork.

I sometimes stood by that railway wall with Barney sitting on it and watched one of the long goods trains pass. It would be carrying all sorts of things, rails of cattle with their heads out through the sides, but it was nice because they were not packed in. They seemed to have plenty of space. After them a long convoy of farm machinery, all shiny and new and sometimes sacks of grain and then, at the very end of the long goods train, the lonely little guard's van. The guard was always leaning out of the open window space and always waved to me as he faded off into the distance. I often wondered where his home was. Did he live in Cork or Dublin? Did he have a wife and children to welcome him home at night? I wondered, did he have homecure bacon and cabbage for his meal? Poor man, of course if he lived in one of the big cities he may not have a place for a pig, but he seemed happy enough. Some guards would be puffing a pipe and taking in the countryside.

When the meadow that grew on the slopes was ready, Mick Neville, Larry Brazil and Uncle Jim would cut it all down with a scythe. This had a long, wooden handle and a long, sharp blade. I am sure it was hard work but they helped each other, then they would have a hand rake to scoop it all up; they would bundle it all out over the ditch and into our field until each one of them brought the donkey and cart and took their own share home and made it into a big stack at the back of the outhouses.

Of course, the passenger trains were few and far between in those days. I know that when I was on holidays from school, grandmother would tell me the times of the different trains. In the morning, I think, about 9.30 a.m., the Cork train would pass on its way up to Dublin. Sometimes I would know someone that would be on it, so Barney and I would be in our spot to give them a wave. People on the trains were always very good to wave. The one o'clock train coming down from Dublin would thunder its way under the high, railway bridge. I remember waiting for it one day to give Mollie Cleary a good wave on her way home from Dublin. Mr and Mrs Cleary were with me. When Mollie put her head out the window, Mr

Cleary shouted, 'There's Mol,' and he was waving his walking stick at the train. Mrs Cleary and I jumped up and down and hugged each other. That was what was always so nice. If someone was coming home from Dublin or England, some of their family would stand at the nearest railway bridge to give them a welcome home wave and, of course, another member of the family would be waiting at Kilmallock station with either the horse and trap or the donkey and cart and what a happy journey home that would be, with all the talking that would be done.

My big day for waiting for the Dublin train would be the day Auntie Peg would be coming home from England. She would have travelled overnight on the boat from Liverpool. Her journey would have really started in Manchester. Grandmother always worried about the long journey she would have before her, but we would be all very excited on that day. This was another time my hair would have been put in ringlets and my best dress and shoes were put on. Mother or Uncle Jim would set off in the horse and trap to Kilmallock station. Grandmother would tell me the time to go up to my spot by the wall with, of course, Barney in tow. I would stand there looking over the railway tracks towards Knocklong. I knew Uncle Maurice and Auntie Kit's farm was a few miles over the track and the train ran through their lands and that my cousins would be all lined along the ditch to wave to Auntie Peg. The next second I would be up on my toes. I would spot the big train heading towards Ballinscaula Bridge, a big trail of smoke and the train would be out under the bridge. I would be gazing like mad for her. I would soon know which lady was my Auntie Peg because she would have her head out the window. She always wore very pretty hats. One hand would be holding on to the hat and the other hand would be waving mad at me. Auntie's hand waving and the train would soon have gone out of sight. Barney and I would run as fast as we could down that little stretch of road to grandmother's house to give her the good news that Auntie Peg was definitely on the train. Grandmother and I would have a last check at the bedroom that was ready for her. I remember the lovely lace edges to the pillowcases and the top sheet that folded back to the lovely creamy, heavy crocheted quilt. The wooden-boarded bedroom floor would have been scrubbed white. Just a little fancy homemade rug by the bed and always a nice bunch of roses from the garden in a vase usually on the window ledge. Mother would have put the dinner well on the go before she would have left for the railway station. We would have a peep at it to see all was well. Under grandmother's instructions I would put one of the best cloths on the table and set it ready for dinner. So from then on every horse and trap we would hear in the distance, I would run out to see if Auntie Peg was arriving and, when she did arrive, there was great hugging and kissing.

She arrived with her big suitcase and matching hat box. She always dressed so nice and was such a fun-loving person. She was so kind too; we would all get some gift. There was always roast chicken and all the trimmings for dinner that day, as far as I can remember. I loved going with her to the bedroom while she unpacked, she always had such pretty dresses. Later on in the day Auntie Kit, Nell and Doris would come, dad and sometimes Uncle Maurice. So while all the adults were talking we would whisper to auntie to ask if we could go and look at her fashions in the bedroom. She always smiled and said yes, but to be careful with her hats. Well, off into the bedroom we would go and close the door. We would try on a big hat in turn, then have a turn of a little dainty hat, then some hats would have a veil that would come down over your face. There was her fox fur but we could not fathom out why this was almost black. We would stretch it out on the bed, until it looked like a fox all right but we had never seen one that colour. Then we decided that they must have some very dark-coloured foxes in England. Of course, we tried it on in turns and, with her high heels that we fell in and out of, we would be in the midst of a wonderful world of make believe of being grown-up ladies. The bedroom door would open and it would be mother or Auntie Kit getting quite cross with us and making us put everything back tidily, but it was great fun.

15

Growing Up Fast

By Christmas 1944 I was very involved in caring for grandmother who was now getting very frail.

Mother would have liked me to have gone to the vocational convent in Kilmallock and I would have loved to have followed some of my friends there, but in those days it cost a lot of money and I being the first one out of the nest, it would have been such a strain for mom and dad to pay for me. Grandmother was sad about this too, because she always said I was such a chatterbox and good to remember whatever I was told and that I would have done well at the convent. However, I was not all that upset when everyone stopped talking about it; I was very happy to look after grandmother full time. Mother came as often as she could. Our last new baby girl, Eileen Ellen, was beautiful and Mary was beginning to help mother with her. Auntie Kit and my cousins Nell, Doris and Hanna May came to visit or stay for a couple of days when on holidays, but that was not as often as I would have liked.

I would make a fine fire in the morning to warm the cold kitchen then feed the hens, chickens and pig, whom I often washed to look clean. I'd then follow the two goats to milk them as grandmother always believed it was very good milk because the goats ate lots of good herbs. I never liked it and was glad to go each evening to Halpin's for cows' milk. When I was able to tell grandmother that the kitchen was lovely and warm and the little grate in her bedroom had a nice red glow showing, I would start to wash her and rub ointment or oil to her poor creaky bones. We had a special way of going through each stage which made it all easy for us both. When I had her fully dressed, I would get her two walking sticks, help her up on her feet and hold her until she got control of the walking sticks, we would start off the slow walk out of the bedroom, across the stone kitchen floor until I had seen her seated safely in her armchair. I would then place a cloth on her shoulders, while I brushed her lovely long, white hair, rolled it up in coils at the back, kept together with lots of hairpins and the last finishing-off bit was two nice combs at each side of the centre back.

Uncle Jim was out at work except for Sunday. It was still a lovely day for family visits. The doctor came every so often and was now giving grandmother some pills for her heart. The priest came to give grandmother Holy Communion. I knew how to set up the kitchen table with a lovely lace cloth that almost reached the floor, a blessed candle in its strong holder and a little fancy glass bowl with spring water in it covered by a white, folded cloth, for the priest to wash his hands. It was Father Leahy and we always looked forward to his visits. He always had a cup of tea with us before he left.

The year 1945 seemed to soon come around. As far as I can remember it was a lovely summer August that brought the end of the war. This brought great joy for everyone. Grandmother had said so many rosaries for peace.

However, September came with such sadness. It was the morning of the 11th that Grandmother started looking very ill and Uncle Jim asked Mick Neville to go on his bicycle for the doctor and priest. I washed her face and hands and settled her bedclothes. I was very upset. It was not long before mother, Auntie Kit, Auntie Mary and Uncle Bill came. We were trying to give her drinks, but she was very confused and I heard the doctor say, 'There's not a puff left in her heart.'

I always remember how kind mum and dad were to me. They seemed to know exactly how upset I was. Grandmother died next day, 12 September. That night she was taken into church and next day she was buried at Athneasy with grand-father. All that side I tried to shut out, I wanted to remember the very special grandmother we were so lucky to have in our lives.

I went back home to Ballingaddy. Uncle Jim now lived on his own at the bridge in grandmother's cottage. I loved being so much again with my sisters, Mary, Peg and Little Nell as we called our little toddler, but I knew that time was not standing still and that I would be seventeen my next birthday. Jobs were very few, even for girls or boys that had done their leaving certificate at high school. Ireland had far more priests, nuns, nurses, teachers and whatever else, than they needed, so for a long time trainloads of young people were leaving for America or England, but mostly England in our day.

For the time being mother was glad of my help at home because twins were born into our home again, this time a boy and a girl, Michael and Noreen. They needed so much nursing and care. Poor Noreen lived only a few weeks, although she was the biggest. We were all so sad the day of her little funeral. It was very like the first twins, Paddy and John, when I was small. Now we were very worried in case we would lose Michael also as he was only two and a half pounds, when he was born, but thank God he came to stay and is now a fine man.

Brigid Maguire and I seemed to see little of each other after leaving school, but we had chats about finding jobs in Dublin. That was never looked on as a good idea by our families.

Lots of letters passed between mother and Auntie Peg, who was my godmother and, of course, I loved her very much, also her husband, Uncle Sam. It was decided that I would go to England to her. Although the war was over, passports and identity cards were still in use between Ireland and England. All the form filling went on for a couple of months, until one day my passport, ID and sailing ticket came all in a big, brown envelope. As I tipped them out on the table to have a good look at them, I remember all went very quiet around the supper table that night. Mary and Peg were asking how long I was going for and remarks like 'Do most people go to England when they grow up?' Mum and dad tried to give them answers in between talking about how great it would be when I would come home on holiday. Mother got busy getting me new clothes, shoes and all she felt I would need for my first big step out into the world. I went about the last few days saying goodbye to aunts, uncles, cousins and all the lovely families I loved so much around Ballinscaula Bridge. There were hugs and tears and lots of good advice. I paid a visit to grandmother's and grandfather's grave and our three little babies and asked them to help me.

With my seventeenth birthday only weeks behind me, the morning of 6 November 1946 came and I lay awake thinking of the journey I was about to start that day. My suitcase was packed. The atmosphere at home seemed to have changed that morning, everyone was helping me, I was feeling lonely but did not want anyone to know. The awful goodbye took place. Mary and Peg clung to me. Nell and Mick were too small to understand. Dad wiped my eyes with his handkerchief, although his own were full up. He warned me if I felt I could not settle to come home, that I would get a job somewhere.

The horse and trap was ready at the front gate. Mother and I set off for Kilmallock station and the usual sight in those days. The station was full of young boys and girls all heading off like me to a new country to start our grown-up life. I had a new, deep-gold-coloured coat and a dark brown jockey hat which was very fashionable at the time; a gold ribbon tied back my long hair, new brown shoes and silk stockings. A little black, velvet bag with a running string round the wrist of my left hand had my money in it and passport and ID card. Mother had a five pound note broken into change for I had to pay each port on my journey in stages, no holiday shops to pay your fare all the way then.

The big train from Cork thundered down the line with lots of young girls and boys looking sad inside the windows. They had got on at all the small stations on the way down. Mother and I hugged and hugged. Mrs Lynch, a lady we knew well, took my arm and sat me next to her on the train. She was going on a visit to Dublin. Mother waved me out of sight and a band was playing on the station the wartime song, 'Wish Me Luck As You Wave Me Goodbye.'

As we sped towards Ballinscaula, Mr and Mrs Cleary, Mollie and Larry Brazil, Mick Halpin and Uncle Jim were all there waving to me. It was so strange. I was the one now sitting on the train. Before we got to Knocklong my cousins were also lined up waving to me. Mrs Lynch was so nice to me all the way. She bought me lunch on the train, the first time I had eaten out, but I was trying not to be rude despite having to force it down. I was so lonely and felt so alone and wondered what would lie ahead of me.

The trains took a long time in those days and it was very dark when we got to Dublin's King's Bridge as it was then called. Petrol rationing was still on, so it was hansom cabs lined up at

107

the station, ready to take people wherever they wanted to be taken. Although lonely I was keeping a close check on my money for the journey from Kilmallock to Manchester Central Station. I had a pen and pad in my little black bag.

Mrs Lynch had booked into some big hotel with friends, horsy people. All the boys and girls like me had to go to guest houses at Westland Row, near that station, to spend the night. Mrs Lynch saw me to the door of a hansom cab. I checked how much it would cost, 3/6, which I took from my little bag. A few more girls and I checked into a guest house. It was ten shillings for a light meal, bed, and breakfast the next morning. I was very tired and lonely, said my prayers, washed and went to bed, my little black bag still on my wrist in case I would lose it. I did not sleep very well, there was too much buzzing around in my head.

Next morning it was up about 7 a.m., got ready, made things tidy, ticked the ten shillings off my list and, with the rest of the people marched down to the station, got on the train and in very little time we got a glimpse of the sea and the big boat waiting for us. We were told to have sailing tickets, passports and IDs ready and, carrying a heavy suitcase for the first time, I trudged up the gangway in the crowd and after all the checking in, I sat next to a man, woman and baby who were making their new home in England.

The boat was now moving, I walked out on to the deck and had a sad look at our lovely Irish hills, now looking further away. The boat was swaying a bit and my stomach did not like it. I went back and sat down. I felt so alone now. All I wanted was for that boat to hurry up. I would not have my loved ones at home in Ballingaddy, so the sooner I was with my god-mother, Auntie Peg, and her lovely husband Uncle Sam, the better.